"Learning a language, modern or ancient, requires that we engage every component of our human language acquisition abilities. For too long ancient languages were taught more like math than languages. The focus was on paradigms and piecemeal analysis. Tools like Scheumanns' *According to Their Kinds* allow us to break free from the worn out grammar-translation models and engage students with stimuli rooted in research on how we acquire languages. This well-designed visual resource recognizes that memory utilizes sense-based cues to acquire vocabulary. I am sure that *According to Their Kinds* will serve teachers and students extremely well, resulting in deeper comprehension and longer retention of Biblical Hebrew."

    Robert D. Holmstedt, Professor of Biblical Hebrew and Ancient West Semitic Languages, University of Toronto; co-author, *Beginning Biblical Hebrew: A Grammar and Illustrated Reader*

"*According to Their Kinds* is a splendid resource for moving Hebrew learners away from thinking about vocabulary as merely English glosses toward broader cognitive concepts. The integration of words, clauses, and images serves to reinforce better understanding of Hebrew language. Furthermore, the chapter groupings are ideal for conceptualizing the relationships between similar terms and ideas. This tool will help beginning, intermediate, and even advanced students find renewed enjoyment in studying Hebrew vocabulary."

    Chip Hardy, Associate Professor of Old Testament & Semitic Languages, Southeastern Baptist Theological Seminary; author, *Exegetical Gems from Biblical Hebrew*

"If we're not careful, with resources like Picture Hebrew and *According to Their Kinds*, learning Hebrew vocabulary might actually become intuitive and enjoyable. We, Biblical Hebrew teachers, won't stand for that! For those teachers of the language who, however, want their students to learn more and suffer less, I highly recommend this resource."

    Jeremiah J. Davidson, Rector and Hebrew Professor, The Pastors School at First Baptist Church of Atibaia, Brazil

"Learning Hebrew through traditional Hebrew-word-to-English-word vocabulary cards is monotonous, time-consuming work that leaves students translating into English rather than reading Hebrew. *According to Their Kinds*, a topically organized visual dictionary of Biblical Hebrew, helps students to think in Hebrew (and expedites the vocabulary acquisition process) by giving students a picture to associate the meaning directly with the Hebrew word, rather than using English as a gateway. A Biblical text is provided to clarify the meaning and give an additional anchor for the memory. Hebrew students and teachers who use this resource will give thanks for the Scheumanns' labors!"

    John C. Beckman, Associate Professor of Old Testament, Bethlehem College & Seminary; author, *Williams' Hebrew Syntax* 3rd ed. (Revised and Expanded)

"Mastering the vocabulary of the Hebrew Bible has always been a problem for students. Picture Hebrew is an important advance in the teaching of the vocabulary of the Hebrew Bible and is distinguished from previous attempts by combining visual and conceptual aspects of lexical items. By grouping words into conceptual categories, students make connections between semantically related words in ways that stimulate the learning and retention of vocabulary items. The beautiful pictures allow students to experience the realia of ancient Israel. In this way, students are able to glimpse the alterity of the world and the world-view of the biblical text. As a companion to the electronic app of Picture Hebrew, *According to their Kinds* provides students in our digital media culture a relevant and effective means to acquire the vocabulary of the Hebrew Bible."

Jacobus A. Naudé and Cynthia L. Miller-Naudé, Senior Professors, Department of Hebrew, University of the Free State, South Africa

"The more senses we can engage in the study of the biblical languages the better! I hope students will be helped to learn Hebrew vocabulary by this creative and visually engaging resource."

James M. Hamilton, Professor of Biblical Theology, The Southern Baptist Theological Seminary

"Thank you to Picture Hebrew for another useful resource, this one for reviewing the most common vocabulary items in the Hebrew Bible in a way that does not use English glosses as the primary interface, and grouping them into categories for easier recall. The use of pictures allows the learning to remain in Hebrew, so key for effective internalizing of the language."

Brian Schultz, Associate Professor of Biblical & Theological Studies, Fresno Pacific University

"This is a brilliant tool for acquiring and for reviewing Hebrew vocabulary—concise, well-organized, and visually engaging. I would highly recommend it for self-study as well as for use in any style of Hebrew classroom."

Sarah Lynn Baker, Lecturer in Hebrew Language and Literature, The University of Texas at Austin

"Scheumann and Scheumann's *According to Their Kinds* is an accessible and well thought-out pedagogical tool. Instead of boring word-lists, students are presented with clear and beautiful images that illustrate vocabulary—engaging different parts of the brain and encouraging natural language learning. *According to Their Kinds* will be an indispensable resource for first-year Hebrew students."

John Screnock, Research Fellow in Hebrew Bible, Faculty of Oriental Studies at University of Oxford

"I know of no comparable resource for helping students internalize Biblical Hebrew vocabulary. The vivid pictures help connect Hebrew words with the real world rather than with an English gloss, thus aligning with how people normally learn languages. The method is tested; the results are sure."

Jason S. DeRouchie, Research Professor of Old Testament and Biblical Theology, Midwestern Baptist Theological Seminary; author, *How to Understand and Apply the Old Testament*

"We naturally acquire language coincidentally and contextually, first by hearing sounds and then associating those sounds with meaning in context we see and experience. More formally, parents may use a "wordbook" with their infant where a word or phrase is attached to a picture. When parents read to their small children, those books are full of illustrations that help them associate what they are hearing with concepts. In the quest of acquiring a reading ability in Biblical Hebrew the Scheumanns have provided a resource so much more effective than flashcards with a Hebrew word on one side and an English gloss on the other. They offer a tool that associates words with an icon to aid in visualizing the concept as well as with an example of its use in context. *According to Their Kinds* is a gift to anyone wishing to learn to read and study Jesus' Bible."

Paul Ferris, Professor of Hebrew Bible Emeritus, Bethel Seminary

"*According to Their Kinds* is optimized to help you log information into long-term memory. A number of associative strategies are employed for this purpose. In particular, this Biblical Hebrew dictionary is unique in providing illustrations for nearly every entry. Additionally, many of those illustrations are based on recognizable Bible passages and characters, each one accompanied by a sentence based on actual biblical text. Finally, the grouping of words according to semantic domains, and often in synonym/antonym pairs, helps cement the meaning of words in relation to others in the language system. I highly recommend this dictionary as a learning tool for all students of Biblical Hebrew. Even those who have already learned much Hebrew vocabulary by other means will be able to see and remember Hebrew words in a new way."

Jacques E. J. Boulet, PhD. Biblical Hebrew Grammar and Linguistics, University of Toronto

"*According to Their Kinds* is a fantastic resource that brings Biblical Hebrew vocabulary to life in a new way. Recommended for students who want to expand their vocabulary and strengthen the direct link between a concept and its Hebrew word without dependence on English as a medium. Clear contextualized illustrations and example sentences from the biblical text make this a great learning tool for really internalizing the language instead of memorizing lists of words."

Bethany Case, Linguist Missionary, Equatorial Guinea

"The Scheumanns have created a beautiful book for learning Biblical Hebrew vocabulary. Nouns and verbs dominate, but adverbs and adjectives are also included. The artwork is beautiful, all in black and white, which keeps costs amazingly low. Some drawings illustrate ancient culture where possible, though sometimes abstract symbols are used for more abstract terms. Four illustrations and words appear per page, with translations at the bottom. This facilitates focusing on Hebrew language rather than translating. Nouns include both singular and plural forms, which are essential to learning the real words. Grammatical terms are given in Hebrew and English, which allows teachers to teach grammar and remain in the language. The vocabularies are arranged in semantic domains, which allows learners to learn and teachers to teach vocabulary more naturally. Each word includes a Scripture quote that gives contextual learning. Words occurring 100+ times are included. I heartily recommend this book for students and teachers."

Lee M. Fields, Professor of Bible, Mid-Atlantic Christian University; author, *Hebrew for the Rest of Us*

"I dreamed of creating a resource like this for many years; the Scheumanns have made my dream a reality. With gripping images, biblical-contextual examples, and helpful thematic categorizations, this tool is for everyone who desires to truly internalize Biblical Hebrew vocabulary. I eagerly await a second volume!"

Marcus A. Leman, PhD. Old Testament, The Southern Baptist Theological Seminary

According to Their Kinds

A Biblical Hebrew Picture Dictionary

Jesse R. Scheumann
Merissa Scheumann

GlossaHouse
Wilmore, KY
www.GlossaHouse.com

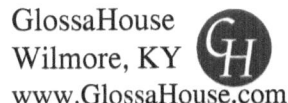

According to Their Kinds:
A Biblical Hebrew Picture Dictionary

Copyright © 2019 by Jesse R. Scheumann and Merissa Scheumann
Illustration copyright © 2019 by Merissa Scheumann
Published by GlossaHouse, LLC

All rights reserved. No part of this work may be reproduced or transmitted in any form or by any means, electronic or mechanical, including photocopying and recording, or by means of any information storage or retrieval system, except as may be expressly permitted by the 1976 Copyright Act or in writing from the publisher. Requests for permission should be addressed in writing to:

>GlossaHouse, LLC
>110 Callis Circle
>Wilmore, KY 40390

Publisher's Cataloging-in-Publication Data

173 pages ; 23cm — (HA'ARETS, Picture Hebrew)

ISBN: 978-1942697930 and 978-1942697602
Library of Congress Control Number: 2019953183

Cover design: Brian Fergus
Cover images: Merissa Scheumann

Printed in the United States of America

www.glossahouse.com

To our former Hebrew students,
and many more to come,
we have toiled joyfully with you in mind.

HA'ARETS

HEBREW & ARAMAIC ACCESSIBLE RESOURCES
FOR EXEGETICAL AND THEOLOGICAL STUDIES

SERIES EDITORS

TRAVIS WEST   JESSE R. SCHEUMANN

GlossaHouse
Wilmore, KY
www.glossahouse.com

HA'ARETS

The Hebrew word הָאָרֶץ means "the earth, the land." It refers to the entirety of the physical world we see and touch and live upon. It is the creation of God, a gift for sustaining life and gladdening the heart, and it is the primary space of God's self-revelation. The HA'ARETS series—Hebrew & Aramaic Accessible Resources for Exegetical and Theological Studies—is an innovative curriculum suite offering resources that participate in the life-giving richness of הָאָרֶץ. The suite offers affordable and innovative print and electronic resources including grammars, readers, specialized studies, and other exegetical materials that encourage and foster the exegetical use of biblical Hebrew and Aramaic for the world and the global church.

ACKNOWLEDGMENTS

This book is the culmination of five years of work. It began with frantic sketches on 3" x 5" cards traced in marker before our first child arrived in April 2014. We had exhausted the available Hebrew picture resources at the time, and we wanted something for the most frequent vocabulary. We showed those (now) embarrassing illustrations to our classmates at a Hebrew ulpan that summer, and surprisingly some expressed interest in getting a set of cards for themselves. We then launched the first of three different renditions of the flashcards to bring them to the public in 2017. Even the third rendition has been through three separate editions, as we have revised all of the drawings based on user feedback.

Our best feedback has come from our own students. We would like to thank the TBI classes of 2014–2017, the PH class of 2017–2018, and the Sattler College class of 2018–2019. Our Plumfund supporters in 2017 enabled us to make high-quality digital scans of the third rendition of the drawings. Our Kickstarter backers in 2018 empowered us to launch an app to reach a larger audience and receive even more feedback. And our parents have supported us every step of the way. Thank you!

Cody Hinkle was the first one (we took seriously) to suggest that we combine the pictures into a book. He gave very valuable constructive criticism at the conceptual stage and at later stages of the book creation, as did Brian Schultz, Benjamin Kantor, Marcus Leman, Sarah Baker, Cam Hamm, Caleb Smoker, and Bethany Case. As Hebrew teachers, they flagged a number of errors for us, and they helped us mold the book into a more pedagogically-sound language resource.

Many other Hebrew scholars gave generously of their time to review a mostly-finalized book draft. To those who endorsed this book, we are

Acknowledgments

deeply grateful. Several gave us comments for improvement. We thank Jacobus Naudé, Cynthia Miller-Naudé, Robert Holmstedt, Kevin Chau, John Beckman, Bernard Levinson, Lee Fields, Jacques Boulet, and John Screnock. Once again, the design, style, and layout of the book, and even some drawings, improved from their remarks. While we acknowledge all of these people in these last two paragraphs for their positive impact, let the reader understand that if any lack remains, the regrettable blame rests solely at our feet.

We would also like to thank some of our current/former students who gave critical feedback on many aspects of this dictionary. These include Lois Friesen, Blair Johnson, Timothy Miller, Christina Boyum, Tyler Foster, Annemarie Metcalf, Matthew Baugher, Bryant Miller, Meredith Nyberg, Maykel Saad, Joy Weiler, and Austin Lapp. Your feedback from the perspective of a user in our target audience was invaluable. Thank you so much!

Finally, it is no perfunctory act to acknowledge God, since "in him we live and move and have our being" (Acts 17:28). Our sincere prayer is, "Not to us, O LORD, not to us, but to your name give glory, for the sake of your steadfast love and faithfulness" (Ps 115:1).

CONTENTS

Abbreviations 12

Transliteration 13

Preface 14

1 The Created Order 19

1.1 Heavens and Earth 20

1.2 Metals and Stone 26

1.3 Plants and Animals 28

1.4 Time and Seasons 34

2 The Human Order 39

2.1 Humans and Anatomy 40

2.2 Food 48

2.3 Clothing 52

3 The Social Order 57

3.1 Family and Tribe 58

3.2 Personal Interactions 64

3.3	Worship/Cultic	70
3.4	People, Law, and Covenant	82
3.5	Lands and Warfare	90
3.6	Education	98

4 The Constructed Order 103

| 4.1 | Building and Travel | 104 |
| 4.2 | Measurement and Numbers | 110 |

5 Word Groups 121

5.1	Movement Verbs	122
5.2	Action and Stative Verbs	128
5.3	Derived Binyanim	136
5.4	Pronouns	144
5.5	Prepositions	148
5.6	Question Words	152
5.7	English Translations	154

Glossary 156

English Index 166

ABBREVIATIONS

ADJ	=	adjective (modifies a noun)
ADV	=	adverb (modifies a verb)
c	=	common (gender)
f	=	feminine (gender)
HI	=	Hif'il (a verbal stem, often for causing an action)
HSTFL	=	Hishtafel (a verbal stem with only one root: חוה)
HTP	=	Hitpa'el (a verbal stem, often reflexive)
imp	=	imperative (conjugation for giving commands)
inf	=	infinitive (a verbal noun that does not inflect)
m	=	masculine (gender)
N	=	noun
NI	=	Nif'al (a verbal stem, often passive)
p	=	plural
PI	=	Pi'el (a verbal stem, often for causing a state)
PREP	=	preposition
Q	=	Qal (the default verbal stem, sometimes called Pa'al)
s	=	singular
vyqtl	=	vayyiqtol (conjugation for narrative past tense)
1	=	first person ("I, we")
2	=	second person ("you")
3	=	third person ("he," "she," "they")
או	=	אוֹ	=	"or"
כג	=	כִּנּוּי גּוּף	=	"pronoun"
ו	=	וְ	=	"and"
פ	=	פּוֹעַל	=	"verb"
שע	=	שֵׁם עֶצֶם	=	"noun"
שת	=	שֵׁם תּוֹאַר	=	"adjective"
תפ	=	תּוֹאַר פּוֹעַל	=	"adverb"

TRANSLITERATION

The transliteration we use is non-technical and is meant to be intuitive to a broad audience. We present the major Hebrew dialect spoken today in Israel.[1] However, this is by no means a universal practice for reading Biblical Hebrew. Professors with another preference should provide their own pronunciation guide.

Alef	א	ʾ (glottal stop) as in uh ʾoh[2]	*Lamed*	ל	l as in **l**ake
Bet	בּ	**b** as in **b**oy	*Mem*	מ\ם	**m** as in **m**an
Vet	ב	**v** as in **v**ase	*Nun*	נ\ן	**n** as in **n**oon
Gimel	ג\גּ	**g** as in **g**oat	*Samex*	ס	**s** as in **s**eed
Dalet	ד\דּ	**d** as in **d**og	*Ayin*	ע	ʾ as in uh ʾoh
He	ה	**h** as in **h**at	*Pe*	פּ	**p** as in **p**ie
Vav	ו	**v** as in **v**ase	*Fe*	פ\ף	**f** as in **f**ish
Zayin	ז	**z** as in **z**oo	*Tsade*	צ\ץ	**ts** as in ca**ts**
Xet	ח	**x** as in Ba**ch**	*Qof*	ק	**q** as in Ira**q**
Tet	ט	**t** as in **t**oy	*Resh*	ר	**r** as in **r**ing
Yod	י	**y** as in **y**ak	*Sin*	שׂ	**s** as in **s**eed
Kaf	כּ	**k** as in **k**ey	*Shin*	שׁ	**sh** as in **sh**ed
Xaf	כ\ך	**x** as in Ba**ch**	*Tav*	ת\תּ	**t** as in **t**oy
ָ / ַ / ֲ		**a** as in f**a**ther	ֵי		**ay** as in **aye**
ֵ / ֶ / ֱ		**e** as in b**e**d	ְ		silent/ə as in **e**xcuse
ִי / ִ		**i** as in mach**i**ne			
ֹ / וֹ / ֳ		**o** as in sn**o**w	וֹי		**oy** as in s**oy**
וּ / ֻ		**u** as in fl**u**			

[1] S. Bolozky, "Phonology: Israeli Hebrew," in G. Khan, ed., *Encyclopedia of Hebrew Language and Linguistics*, Vol 3 (Leiden; Boston: Brill, 2013), 113–122. *Alef* and *Ayin* are often unpronounced, in which case they are not transliterated. The vowel letters *Yod* and *He* do not alter vowel sound, so we do not list them in the vowel section.

[2] *Alef* and *Ayin* are only transliterated this way when they begin a word-medial syllable.

PREFACE

Audience and Stages of Use

Acquiring Hebrew vocabulary is often slow and tedious, and yet reading biblical passages is impossible without a large word bank. This dictionary includes all words that occur 100 times or more in the Hebrew Bible, and there are about 50 extra words to round out the vocabulary sections.

According to Their Kinds ushers students into the world of Biblical Hebrew. English is separate and in grayscale at the bottom of the page to keep readers in the target language as much as possible. The vocabulary list is arranged in sections by thematic categories.[1] The pictures proceed from general to specific, as the user scans the page left-to-right and top-to-bottom. There are often correlations between nouns and verbs that are in the same row on facing pages.

We designed this dictionary as an intuitive resource for self-study. It is also an engaging textbook for a beginning or intermediate Hebrew class. I (Jesse) use it in third semester, where I assign a few pages for each class period. Students translate the example sentences for quizzes. In this way, they review the most important vocabulary from first year, while also adding new vocabulary learned in context of the biblical verses.

An intermediate student can start reading the book cover-to-cover, but a beginner should follow three incremental stages of learning. First, there is transliteration at the bottom of the page to aid in reading and memorizing the illustrated Hebrew vocabulary. A sideways caret indicates a non-final accent in the Hebrew word.[2] For transliteration, each stressed syllable has

---

[1] The first four main-section headings are taken from J. D. Pleins with J. Homrighausen, *Biblical Hebrew Vocabulary by Conceptual Categories* (Grand Rapids, MI: Zondervan, 2017). We adapted the sub-sections and moved words based on the needs of our list.

[2] We treat words like מַיִם as monosyllabic with a diphthong. See previous page.

an acute accent mark. There is no audio companion for this book, but it is included for the flashcard app deck, available at glossahouse.com.

Second, after learning a critical mass of words, a student is able to read the short sentences under the verbs. Third, the sentences for non-verb vocabulary present a more challenging opportunity to read Hebrew.

This book is primarily a learning tool and secondarily a reference guide. A number of words were too abstract to illustrate and are listed in section 5.7 with English translations. The glossary and index in the back of the book provide easy reference for all Hebrew word entries.

Principles of Illustration

Non-verb illustrations are simple and generic. Verbs illustrate an iconic usage, and each character is recognizable from picture to picture. Most of the illustrations contain a text box in a particular corner to indicate whether the word is a verb (פ), noun (שע), adjective (שת), adverb (תפ), or pronoun (כג). The following principles guided our illustrations:
- The primary figure is centered, foregrounded, and bolded
- All "movement" flows right to left
- The illustration captures the central/basic sense of the word
  - Literal sense is preferred over metaphorical sense
  - One meaning is preferred over multiple, unless ...
    - A second meaning is on par with the first as central in the semantic range, or
    - A second meaning is unrelated to the first and would otherwise be confusing even in context
- A word with two meanings has the Hebrew word "or" (או) between the illustrations
- A word with one meaning may be illustrated in bold with a solid line separating it and its antonym or a previous scene (given for context)
- Two antonyms with one form each are illustrated in the same picture and separated by the Hebrew word "and" (ו)
- An "or (או) ..." in the bottom-left corner marks a general word that had to be illustrated with a specific example (e.g. stealing for "to sin")

Explanation of Non-Verb Forms

Noun entries list the singular form and, if attested, the plural form (unless the dual is more common). The second form shows that many nouns take irregular endings. We list the gender after most nouns. For nouns with mixed data, we list whichever gender is more often reflected. For nouns with no indication, we leave the gender blank.

All adjectives list both the masculine and feminine singular forms. Listing two forms, as with nouns, helps students naturally absorb patterns of inflection, and it enables them to predict the plural forms.

For every vocabulary entry, we put a backslash between two Hebrew forms of the same word. We separate two different words (synonyms or antonyms) on the same line with a raised dot.

We illustrate only the spatial sense for prepositions, even though most of them have logical extensions. The pictures are designed for beginners who, like children, thrive in absorbing the language as a simple, concrete system. The maturing student who reads biblical texts will pick up on the other uses of these prepositions when they occur in context.

All geographic places that occur over 100 times are included. Each nation's size represents the height of its expansion in a way that does not overlap with another nation.[3] Personal names are not illustrated.

Explanation of Verb Forms

For each verbal entry, we list the 3ms qatal (perfect) and the 3ms yiqtol (imperfect) forms. Under the sentence are four extra forms that are useful to know: infinitive | 2ms imperative | 3ms vayyiqtol | consonantal root.

The rest of this section is technical. Beginning students can skip it. The verb list is derived from roots that occur 100 times or more. Each root is illustrated as Qal if it occurs in that binyan (stem). But many roots are not attested as Qal. In these cases, we illustrate whichever binyan (Nif'al, Pi'el, or Hif'il) occurs most frequently. These words are often best thought of as having approximately the same type of meaning as Qal.

---

[3] We adapted the maps from T. V. Brisco, *Holman Bible Atlas: A Complete Guide to the Expansive Geography of Biblical History* (Nashville, TN: B&H, 1998).

To teach the binyanim system, we illustrate many derived-binyanim words that have a Qal counterpart. Nif'al often has a passive meaning ("be found" vs. Qal "find"). Pi'el often has a causative-state connotation ("consecrate" vs. Qal "be holy"). Hif'il often has a causative-action sense ("proclaim" vs. Qal "hear"). And Hitpa'el often has a definition reflexive of Qal or Pi'el ("boast" vs. Pi'el "praise"). We do not include Hof'al or Pu'al words. We chose to incorporate a derived-binyan word especially if it occurs 100 times or more, or if its meaning is surprising within the binyanim system.

Explanation of Hebrew Sentences

All proper nouns in the sentences are in grayscale to provide an easier reading experience. Each verb-entry sentence is based on the illustrated verse, and the verb is converted into a participle. We did this both to provide another verbal form and to describe the picture as a snapshot of an in-progress action. The default word order for participle clauses is subject-predicate.[4] An asterisk marks the sentences that do not employ a participle for semantic or syntactic reasons.

Each sentence in a non-verb entry is a direct quote from the Hebrew Bible. These sentences are harder to read than the verb entries, because they rarely describe the pictures, and because the predicate is unaltered and thus can be in any conjugation. Sometimes we condensed the verse. We also made a couple changes to standardize spelling: all pausal forms are removed, and the 3fs subject pronoun always appears as הִיא. But other variations—like plene vs. defective spelling and an accent shift to avoid stress clash—are maintained from the Masoretic Text.

The translation of all sentences are our own, and the Bible references in parentheses cite the Hebrew versification. An asterisk indicates each instance when the English reference is different.

---

[4] R. Buth, "Word Order in the Verbless Clause: A Generative-Functional Approach," in C. Miller, ed., *The Verbless Clause in Biblical Hebrew* (Winona Lake, IN: Eisenbrauns, 1999), 79–108.

1
The Created Order

1.1
Heavens and Earth

Heavens and Earth

שָׁמַיִם

וַיְכֻלּוּ הַשָּׁמַיִם וְהָאָרֶץ וְכָל־צְבָאָם

שֶׁמֶשׁ

יֵשׁ רָעָה רָאִיתִי תַּחַת הַשָּׁמֶשׁ

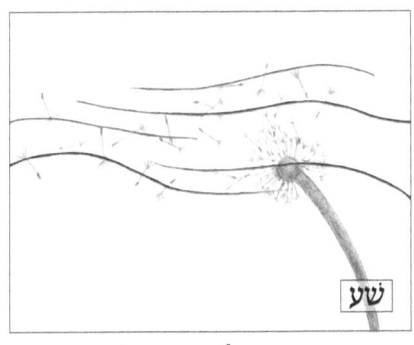

רוּחַ \ רוּחוֹת

וַיּוֹלֶךְ יְהוָה אֶת־הַיָּם בְּרוּחַ קָדִים

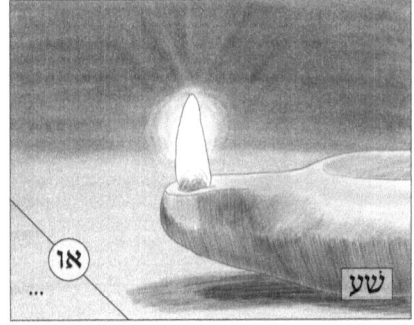

אוֹר

וַיֹּאמֶר אֱלֹהִים יְהִי אוֹר וַיְהִי־אוֹר

---

shamáym
N: heaven, sky (m)
The heavens and the earth and all their host were finished. (Gen 2:1)

shémesh
N: sun (f)
"There is an evil I have seen under the sun." (Eccl 10:5)

rúax / ruxót
N: wind; spirit (f)
YHWH led the sea with an east wind. (Exod 14:21)

ór
N: light (m)
And God said, "Let there be light," and there was light. (Gen 1:3)

 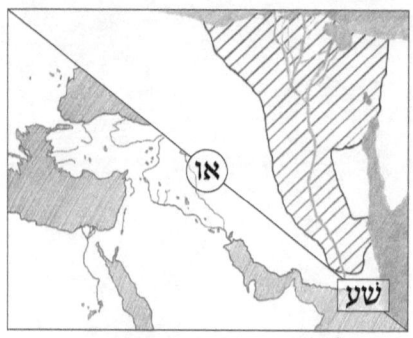

אֶ֫רֶץ \ אֲרָצוֹת צָפוֹן

וַתֵּלַהּ אֶ֫רֶץ מִצְרַיִם וְאֶ֫רֶץ כְּנַ֫עַן כִּי רָעָה אָנֹכִי מֵבִיא מִצָּפוֹן

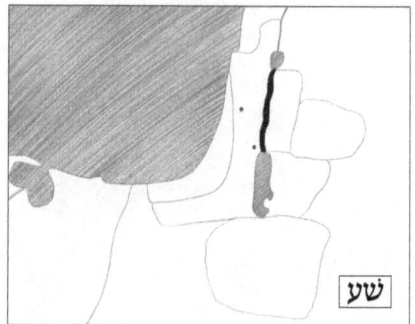 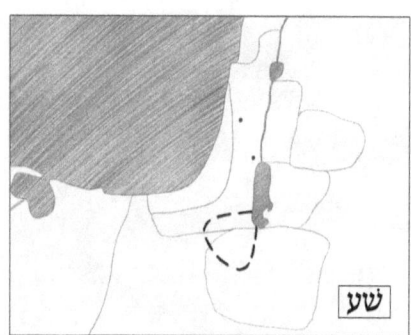

נֶ֫גֶב יַרְדֵּן

וַיִּקַּח יְהוֹשֻׁעַ אֶת־כָּל־הַנֶּ֫גֶב קוּם עֲבֹר אֶת־הַיַּרְדֵּן הַזֶּה

érets / aratsót
N: land; (known) world, earth (f)
The land of Egypt and the land of Canaan languished. (Gen 47:13)

tsafón
N: north
"... because I am bringing a disaster from the north." (Jer 4:6)

négev
N: Negev, arid terrain
And Joshua took all of the Negev. (Josh 11:16)

yardén
N: Jordan (m)
"Get up, cross this Jordan." (Josh 1:2)

Heavens and Earth

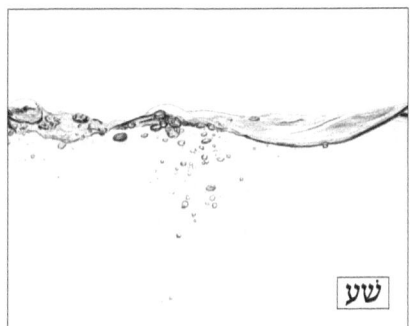

מַיִם

וְאֵין מַיִם לִשְׁתֹּת הָעָם

יָם \ יַמִּים

וַיָּבֹאוּ בְנֵי־יִשְׂרָאֵל בְּתוֹךְ הַיָּם

נַחַל \ נְחָלִים

וָאַשְׁלִךְ אֶל־הַנַּחַל הַיֹּרֵד מִן־הָהָר

נָהָר \ נְהָרוֹת

נָהָר יֹצֵא מֵעֵדֶן לְהַשְׁקוֹת אֶת־הַגָּן

---

máym
N: water (m)
And there was no water for the people to drink. (Exod 17:1)

yám / yamím
N: sea (m)
And the children of Israel went into the midst of the sea. (Exod 14:22)

náxal / nəxalím
N: stream, wadi (m)
"I threw (it) into the stream that goes down from the mountain." (Deut 9:21)

nahár / nəharím
N: river (m)
A river was going out of Eden to water the garden. (Gen 2:9)

מָקוֹם \ מְקוֹמוֹת   שָׂדֶה \ שָׂדוֹת

וַיִּקְרָא אֶת־שֵׁם־הַמָּקוֹם בֵּית־אֵל   וַיָּבֹא עֵשָׂו מִן־הַשָּׂדֶה וְהוּא עָיֵף

אֲדָמָה \ אֲדָמוֹת   מִגְרָשׁ \ מִגְרָשִׁים

וְקַיִן הָיָה עֹבֵד אֲדָמָה   וּמִגְרְשֵׁיהֶם יִהְיוּ לִבְהֶמְתָּם

---

maqóm / məqomót
N: place, location (m)
And he called the name of the place
"Bethel." (Gen 28:19)

sadé / sadót
N: open field (m)
And Esau came in from the field,
and he was tired. (Gen 25:29)

adamá / adamót
N: ground (f)
And Cain was a worker of ground.
(Gen 4:2)

migrásh / migrashím
N: pastureland (m)
"And their pasturelands shall be for
their livestock." (Num 35:3)

Heavens and Earth   25

הַר \ הָרִים

וַיָּבֹא אֶל־הַר הָאֱלֹהִים חֹרֵבָה

מִדְבָּר

וַיְנִעֵם בַּמִּדְבָּר אַרְבָּעִים שָׁנָה

אֵשׁ

וַתִּפֹּל הָאֵשׁ וַתֹּאכַל אֶת־הָעֹלָה

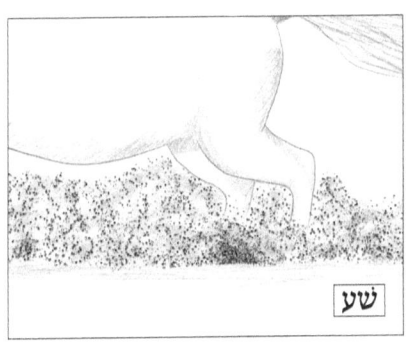

עָפָר

וַיִּיצֶר אֱלֹהִים אֶת־הָאָדָם עָפָר

---

hár / harím
N: mountain (m)
He came to the mountain of God, to Horeb. (Exod 3:1)

midbár
N: wilderness, desert (m)
"He made them wander in the desert forty years." (Num 32:13)

ésh
N: fire (f)
And the fire fell and ate the burnt offering. (1 Kgs 18:38)

afár
N: dust (m)
And God formed the man out of dust. (Gen 2:7)

1.2
Metals and Stone

Metals and Stone

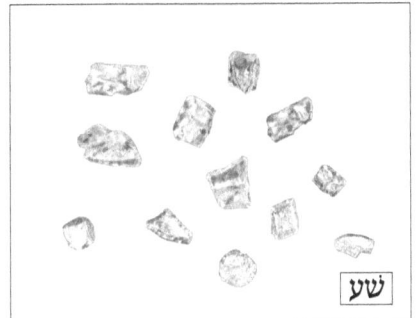

זָהָב
וְאַבְרָם כָּבֵד מְאֹד בַּמִּקְנֶה בַּכֶּסֶף וּבַזָּהָב

כֶּסֶף
הוּשַׁב כַּסְפִּי וְהִנֵּה בְאַמְתַּחְתִּי

אֶבֶן \ אֲבָנִים
וַיִּקְחוּ־אֶבֶן וַיָּשִׂימוּ תַחְתָּיו

נְחֹשֶׁת
וַיַּעַשׂ מֹשֶׁה נְחַשׁ נְחֹשֶׁת

---

zaháv
N: gold (m)
And Abram was very heavy with silver and with gold. (Gen 13:2)

késef
N: silver, money (m)
"My silver has been returned, and here it is in my sack." (Gen 42:28)

éven / avaním
N: stone, rock (f)
They took a stone, and they placed (it) under him. (Exod 17:12)

nəxóshet
N: copper, bronze (f)
And Moses made a serpent of bronze. (Num 21:9)

1.3
Plants and Animals

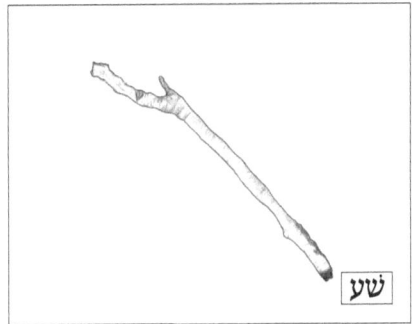

עֵץ \ עֵצִים
וּמֵעֵץ הַדַּעַת טוֹב וָרָע לֹא תֹאכַל

מַקֵּל \ מַקְלוֹת
וַיַּךְ אֶת־הָאָתוֹן בַּמַּקֵּל

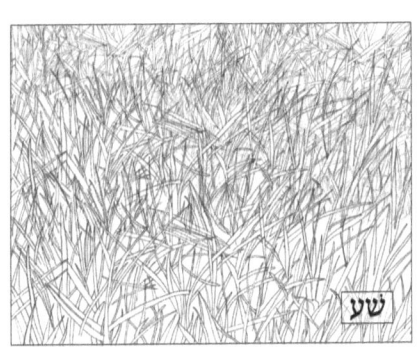

דֶּשֶׁא
בִּנְאוֹת דֶּשֶׁא יַרְבִּיצֵנִי

פֶּרַח \ פְּרָחִים
וַיֹּצֵא מַטֵּה־אַהֲרֹן פֶּרַח

éts / etsím
N: tree, wood (m)
"But from the tree of knowing good and evil you shall not eat." (Gen 2:17)

maqél / maqlót
N: branch, stick (m)
And he struck the donkey with the stick. (Num 22:27)

déshe
N: grass, vegetation (m)
"In pastures of grass he makes me lie down." (Ps 23:2)

pérax / praxím
N: flower, blossom (m)
And the staff of Aaron brought forth a flower. (Num 17:23*)

בְּהֵמָה \ בְּהֵמוֹת   חַיָּה \ חַיּוֹת

מִן־הַבְּהֵמָה מִן־הַבָּקָר וּמִן־הַצֹּאן   כָּל־הַחַיָּה אֲשֶׁר־אִתְּךָ מִכָּל־בָּשָׂר

בָּקָר   צֹאן

וּמֶה קוֹל הַבָּקָר אֲשֶׁר אָנֹכִי שֹׁמֵעַ   וַיְהִי־הֶבֶל רֹעֵה צֹאן

---

bəhemá / bəhemót
N: livestock (f)
"... from the livestock: from the cattle and from the flock." (Lev 1:2)

xayá / xayót
N: animal (f)
"Every animal that is with you of all flesh ..." (Gen 8:17)

baqár
N: cattle, herd (m)
"And what is the voice of the cattle that I am hearing?" (1 Sam 15:14)

tsón
N: flock(s) (m)
And Abel was a shepherd of a flock. (Gen 4:2)

כֶּבֶשׂ \ כְּבָשִׂים   אַיִל \ אֵילִים

וְשָׁחַט אֶת־הַכֶּבֶשׂ הָאָשָׁם   וַיִּשָּׂא אֶת־עֵינָיו וַיַּרְא אַיִל

עֵגֶל \ עֲגָלִים   פַּר \ פָּרִים

וָאַשְׁלִכֵהוּ בָאֵשׁ וַיֵּצֵא הָעֵגֶל הַזֶּה   וְשָׁחַטְתָּ אֶת־הַפָּר לִפְנֵי יְהוָה

---

kéves / kəvasím
N: young ram, sheep (m)
"He shall slaughter the young ram of the guilt offering." (Lev 14:25)

áyl / elím
N: ram (m)
He lifted his eyes, and he saw a ram. (Gen 22:13)

égel / agalím
N: young bull, calf (m)
"I threw it in the fire, and out came this calf." (Exod 32:24)

pár / parím
N: bull (m)
"And you shall slaughter the bull before YHWH." (Exod 29:11)

סוּס \ סוּסִים
וַיָּבֹא נַעֲמָן בְּסוּסוֹ וּבְרִכְבּוֹ

חֲמוֹר \ חֲמוֹרִים
וַתָּקָם וַתִּרְכַּב עַל־הַחֲמוֹר

גָּמָל \ גְּמַלִּים
וַיִּשָּׂא אֶת־נָשָׁיו עַל־הַגְּמַלִּים

עֵז \ עִזִּים
וְהָאִישׁ גָּדוֹל מְאֹד וְלוֹ אֶלֶף עִזִּים

sús / susím
N: horse (m)
And Naaman came with his horse and with his chariot. (2 Kgs 5:9)

xamór / xamorím
N: donkey (m)
She arose and rode on the donkey. (1 Sam 25:42)

gamál / gəmalím
N: camel (m)
And he lifted his wives up on the camels. (Gen 31:17)

éz / izím
N: goat (f)
The man was very great, and he had one thousand goats. (1 Sam 25:2)

Plants and Animals 33

נָחָשׁ \ נְחָשִׁים
וַיֹּאמֶר הַנָּחָשׁ אֶל־הָאִשָּׁה

אַרְיֵה \ אֲרָיוֹת
וַיִּמְצָאֵהוּ אַרְיֵה בַּדֶּרֶךְ וַיְמִיתֵהוּ

עוֹף
וְהָעוֹף אֹכֵל אֹתָם מִן־הַסַּל

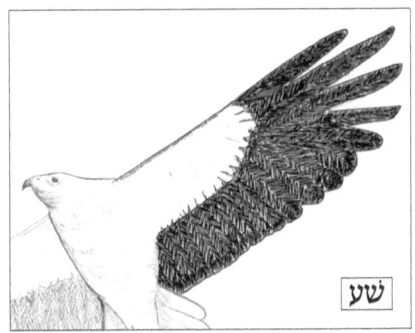

כָּנָף \ כְּנָפַיִם
וָאֶשָּׂא אֶתְכֶם עַל־כַּנְפֵי נְשָׁרִים

naxásh / nəxashím
N: snake (m)
And the snake said to the woman ...
(Gen 3:4)

aryé / arayót
N: lion (m)
A lion found him in the road and
killed him. (1 Kgs 13:24)

óf
N: bird(s) (m)
"And the birds were eating them
from the basket." (Gen 40:17)

kanáf / kənafáym
N: wing; edge (f)
"And I carried you on wings of
eagles." (Exod 19:4)

1.4
Time and Seasons

Time and Seasons

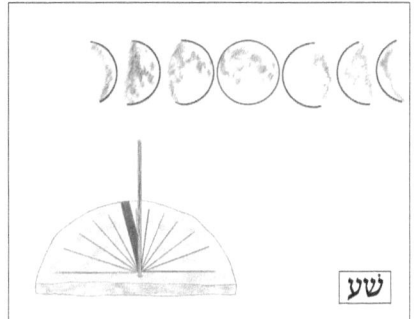 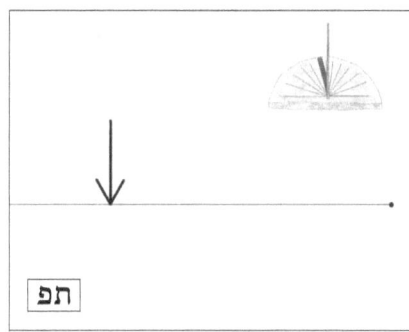

עֵת \ עִתִּים   עַתָּה

וַיֹּאמֶר לָה בֹעַז לְעֵת הָאֹכֶל   עַתָּה יָדַעְתִּי כִּי־גָדוֹל יְהוָה

 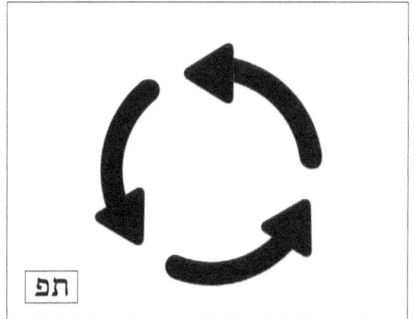

עוֹלָם \ עוֹלָמִים   תָּמִיד

יְהוָה יִמְלֹךְ לְעֹלָם וָעֶד   תֹּאכַל לֶחֶם עַל־שֻׁלְחָנִי תָּמִיד

ét / itím	atá
N: time (f)	ADV: now
And Boaz said to her at the time for food … (Ruth 2:14)	"Now I know that YHWH is great." (Exod 18:11)
olám / olamím	tamíd
N: forever (m)	ADV/ADJ: regular(ly), always
"YHWH will reign forever and ever." (Exod 15:18)	"You shall eat bread at my table regularly." (2 Sam 9:7)

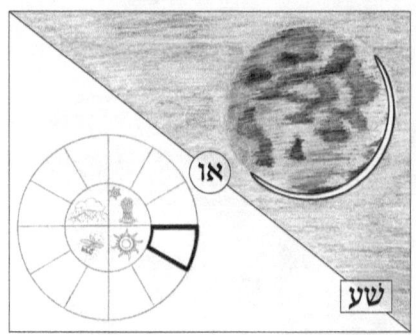

חֹדֶשׁ \ חֳדָשִׁים

וַיֹּאמֶר דָּוִד הִנֵּה־חֹדֶשׁ מָחָר

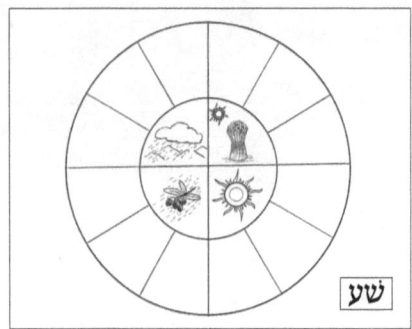

שָׁנָה \ שָׁנִים

אָכְלוּ אֶת־הַמָּן אַרְבָּעִים שָׁנָה

שַׁבָּת \ שַׁבָּתוֹת

וְיוֹם הַשְּׁבִיעִי שַׁבָּת לַיהוָה

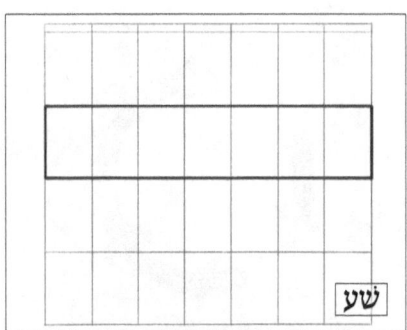

שָׁבוּעַ \ שָׁבֻעוֹת

אִם־נְקֵבָה תֵלֵד וְטָמְאָה שְׁבֻעַיִם

---

shaná / shaním
N: year (f)
They ate the manna for forty years.
(Exod 16:35)

xódesh / xodashím
N: new moon; month (m)
And David said, "Behold, it is a new moon tomorrow." (1 Sam 20:5)

shavúa / shavu'ót
N: week (m)
"If she births a female, she shall be unclean for two weeks." (Lev 12:5)

shabát / shabatót
N: Sabbath, rest (f)
"But the seventh day is a Sabbath to YHWH." (Exod 20:10)

Time and Seasons

יוֹם \ יָמִים

וַיִּקְרָא אֱלֹהִים לָאוֹר יוֹם

לַיְלָה \ לֵילוֹת

וְלַחֹשֶׁךְ קָרָא לָיְלָה

בֹּקֶר \ בְּקָרִים

וַיְהִי בַבֹּקֶר וְהִנֵּה־הִיא לֵאָה

עֶרֶב

וַיְהִי־עֶרֶב וַיְהִי־בֹקֶר יוֹם אֶחָד

---

yóm / yamím
N: day (m)
And God called the light "day."
(Gen 1:5)

láyla / lelót
N: night (m)
And the darkness he called "night."
(Gen 1:5)

bóqer / bəqarím
N: morning (m)
It happened that in the morning,
behold, it was Leah. (Gen 29:25)

érev
N: evening (m)
There was evening and there was
morning, day one. (Gen 1:5)

2
The Human Order

2.1 Humans and Anatomy

Humans and Anatomy   41

אִשָּׁה \ נָשִׁים

יָדַעְתִּי כִּי אִשָּׁה יְפַת־מַרְאֶה אַתְּ

אִישׁ \ אֲנָשִׁים

כֻּלָּנוּ בְּנֵי אִישׁ־אֶחָד

יַלְדָּה \ יְלָדוֹת

קַח־לִי אֶת־הַיַּלְדָּה הַזֹּאת לְאִשָּׁה

יֶלֶד \ יְלָדִים

הַיֶּלֶד אֵינֶנּוּ וַאֲנִי אָנָה אֲנִי־בָא

ísh / anashím
N: man; husband (m)
"All of us are sons of one man."
(Gen 42:11)

ishá / nashím
N: woman; wife (f)
"I know that a woman beautiful in appearance are you." (Gen 12:11)

yéled / yəladím
N: boy (m)
"The boy, he is no more. And I, where am I going?" (Gen 37:30)

yaldá / yəladót
N: girl (f)
"Take for me this girl as a wife."
(Gen 34:4)

אָדָם   שֵׁם \ שֵׁמוֹת

וַיַּרְא כִּי רַבָּה רָעַת הָאָדָם בָּאָרֶץ   וַיִּקְרָא הָאָדָם שֵׁם אִשְׁתּוֹ חַוָּה

נַעַר \ נְעָרִים   זָקֵן \ זְקֵנִים

בֶּן־שְׁבַע־עֶשְׂרֵה שָׁנָה וְהוּא נַעַר   לֵךְ וְאָסַפְתָּ אֶת־זִקְנֵי יִשְׂרָאֵל

---

adám
N: man, humankind; Adam (m)
He saw that great was the evil of man on the earth. (Gen 6:5)

shém / shemót
N: name (m)
And the man called the name of his wife "Eve." (Gen 3:20)

ná'ar / nə'arím
N: young man, lad (m)
... seventeen years old, and he was a young man. (Gen 37:2)

zaqén / zəqením
N: old person, elder (m)
"Go and gather the elders of Israel." (Exod 3:16)

Humans and Anatomy 43

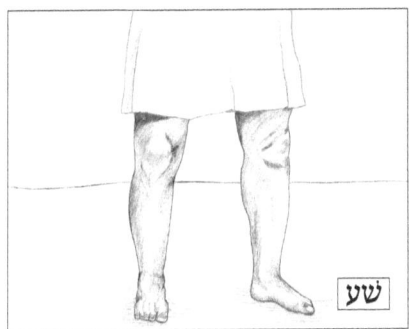

רֶ֫גֶל \ רַגְלַיִם

וְסִיסְרָא נָס בְּרַגְלָיו אֶל־אֹ֫הֶל יָעֵל

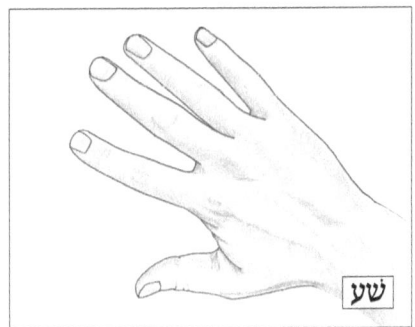

יָד \ יָדַיִם

וְחֶ֫רֶב אֵין בְּיַד־דָּוִד

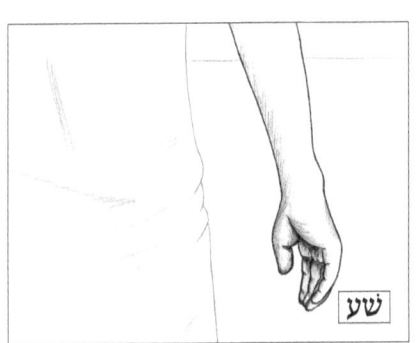

יָמִין

וַיִּשְׁלַח יִשְׂרָאֵל אֶת־יְמִינוֹ

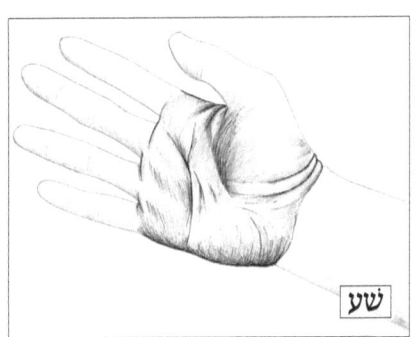

כַּף \ כַּפּוֹת

בְּשִׁמְךָ אֶשָּׂא כַפָּי

---

régel / ragláym
N: leg, foot (f)
And Sisera fled on his feet to the tent of Jael. (Judg 4:17)

yamín
N: right hand, right (m)
And Israel reached out his right hand. (Gen 48:14)

yád / yadáym
N: hand (f)
And there was no sword in the hand of David. (1 Sam 17:50)

káf / kapót
N: palm (f)
"In your name I will lift up my palms." (Ps 63:5*)

רֹאשׁ \ רָאשִׁים
וַהֲסִרֹתִי אֶת־רֹאשְׁךָ מֵעָלֶיךָ

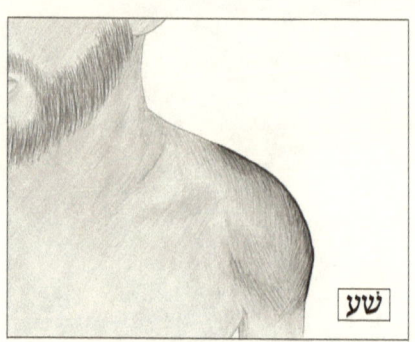

כָּתֵף \ כְּתֵפַיִם
וַיָּשֶׂם אֹתָם עַל כִּתְפֹת הָאֵפֹד

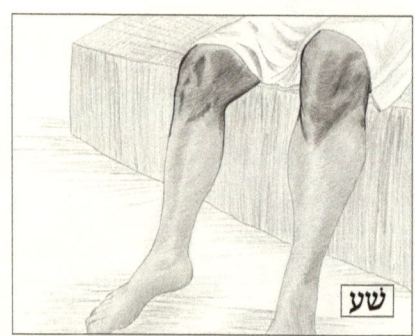

בֶּרֶךְ \ בִּרְכַּיִם
כָּרְעוּ עַל־בִּרְכֵיהֶם לִשְׁתּוֹת מָיִם

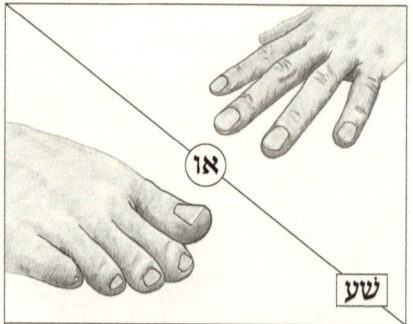

אֶצְבַּע \ אֶצְבָּעוֹת
וַיִּטְבֹּל אֶצְבָּעוֹ בַּדָּם

---

rósh / rashím
N: head (m)
"And I will remove your head from upon you." (1 Sam 17:46)

katéf / kətafáym
N: shoulder (f)
And he placed them on the shoulders of the ephod. (Exod 39:7)

bérex / birkáym
N: knee (f)
They bent down on their knees to drink water. (Judg 7:6)

etsbá / etsba'ót
N: finger; toe (f)
And he dipped his finger in the blood. (Lev 9:9)

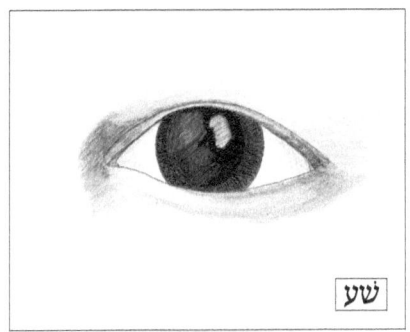
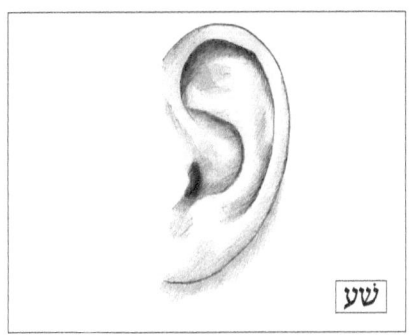

עַיִן \ עֵינַיִם
וְנֹחַ מָצָא חֵן בְּעֵינֵי יְהוָה

אֹזֶן \ אָזְנַיִם
וַיְדַבְּרוּ עַבְדֵי שָׁאוּל בְּאָזְנֵי דָוִד

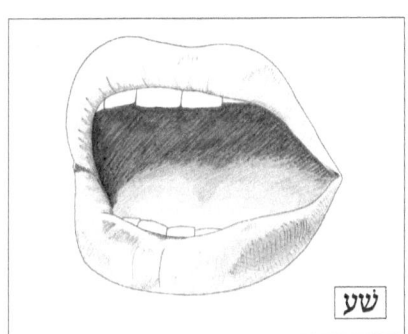
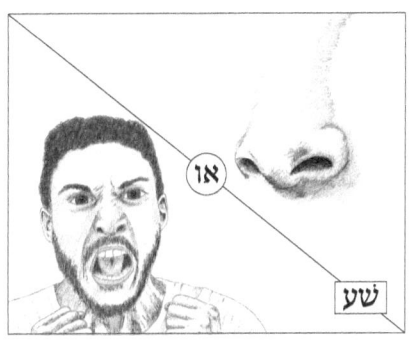

פֶּה
וְעַתָּה לֵךְ וְאָנֹכִי אֶהְיֶה עִם־פִּיךָ

אַף \ אַפַּיִם
וַיִּשְׁתַּחוּ אַפַּיִם אָרְצָה

áyn / enáym
N: eye (f)
But Noah found favor in the eyes of YHWH. (Gen 6:8)

ózen / oznáym
N: ear (f)
And the servants of Saul spoke in the ears of David. (1 Sam 18:23)

pé
N: mouth (m)
"And now, go, and I will be with your mouth." (Exod 4:12)

áf / apáym
N: nose, nostrils; anger (m)
And he bowed down, nostrils to the earth. (Gen 19:1)

פָּנִים

וַיִּפֹּל אַבְרָם עַל־פָּנָיו

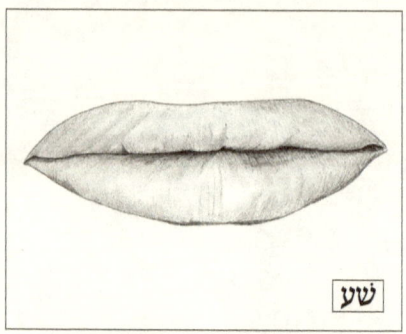

שָׂפָה \ שְׂפָתַיִם

מוֹצָא שְׂפָתֶיךָ תִּשְׁמֹר וְעָשִׂיתָ

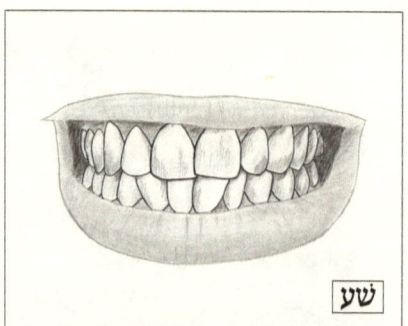

שֵׁן \ שִׁנַּיִם

עַיִן תַּחַת עַיִן שֵׁן תַּחַת שֵׁן

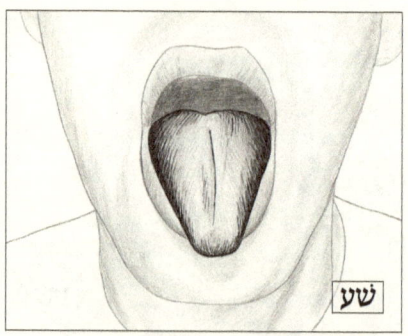

לָשׁוֹן \ לְשׁוֹנוֹת

כִּי כְבַד־פֶּה וּכְבַד לָשׁוֹן אָנֹכִי

---

paním
N: face (f)
And Abram fell on his face.
(Gen 17:3)

safá / sfatáym
N: lip (f)
"What has gone out of your lips you shall keep and do." (Deut 23:24*)

shén / shináym
N: tooth (f)
"... an eye in place of an eye, a tooth in place of a tooth." (Exod 21:24)

lashón / ləshonót
N: tongue (f)
"... because heavy of mouth and heavy of tongue am I." (Exod 4:10)

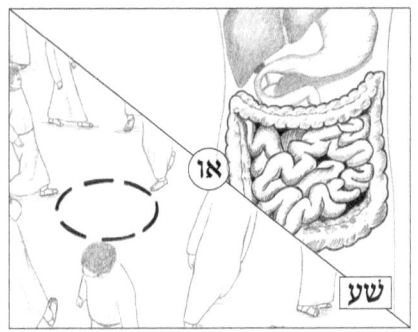

קֶרֶב
הַחֵלֶב הַמְכַסֶּה אֶת־הַקֶּרֶב

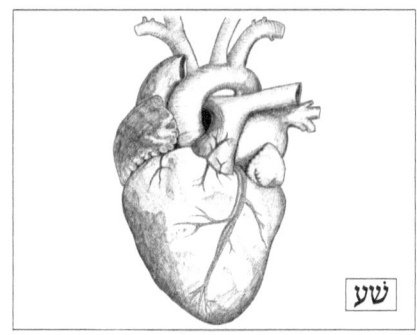

לֵב · לֵבָב
כָּבֵד לֵב פַּרְעֹה מֵאֵן לְשַׁלַּח הָעָם

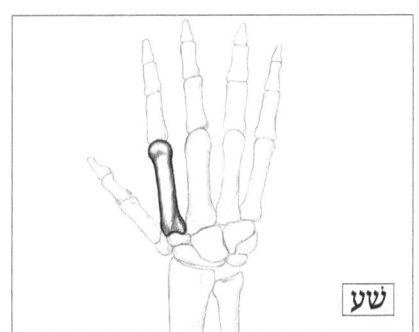

עֶצֶם \ עֲצָמוֹת
זֹאת הַפַּעַם עֶצֶם מֵעֲצָמַי

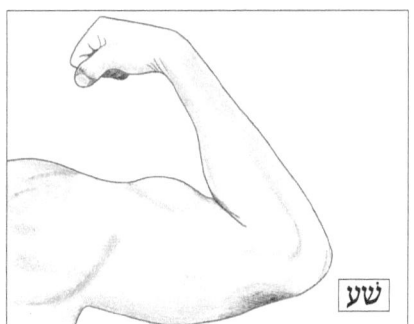

כֹּחַ
הַגִּידָה־נָּא לִי בַּמֶּה כֹּחֲךָ גָדוֹל

---

qérev
N: entrails; midst (m)
"... the fat that covers the entrails." (Exod 29:22)

lév / leváv
N: heart (m)
"Heavy is Pharaoh's heart. He refused to send away the people." (Exod 7:14)

étsem / atsamót
N: bone (f)
"This (woman) is this time bone from my bones." (Gen 2:23)

kóax
N: strength, power (m)
"Tell me, please. How is your strength great?" (Judg 16:6)

2.2
Food

Food

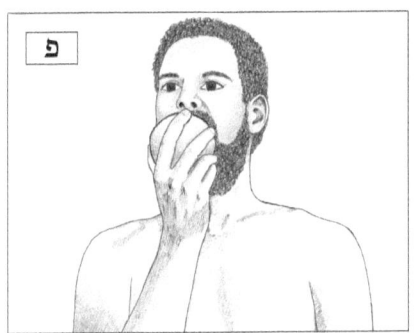

אָכַל \ יֹאכַל
אָדָם אָכַל אֶת־הַפְּרִי

אכל | וַיֹּאכַל | אָכֹל | אֱכֹל

שָׁתָה \ יִשְׁתֶּה
הָעָם שָׁתָה מַיִם מִן־הַצּוּר

שתה | וַיֵּשְׁתְּ | שָׁתֹה | שְׁתוֹת

טָעַם \ יִטְעַם
יוֹנָתָן טָעַם מְעַט דְּבַשׁ

טעם | וַיִּטְעַם | טָעַם | טָעֹם

בָּלַע \ יִבְלַע
מַטֵּה־אַהֲרֹן בָּלַע אֶת־מַטֹּתָם

בלע | וַיִּבְלַע | בְּלַע | בָּלֹעַ

---

axál / yoxál
Q: eat
Adam is eating the fruit.
(Gen 3:6)

shatá / yishté
Q: drink
The people are drinking water from the rock. (Exod 17:6)

taʾám / yitʾám
Q: taste
Jonathan is tasting a little honey.
(1 Sam 14:43)

balá / yivlá
Q: swallow
Aaron's staff is swallowing their staffs. (Exod 7:12)

רָעָב   מִשְׁתֶּה

וַיְהִי רָעָב בָּאָרֶץ וַיֵּרֶד מִצְרַיְמָה   וַיַּעַשׂ לָהֶם מִשְׁתֶּה וַיֹּאכְלוּ וַיִּשְׁתּוּ

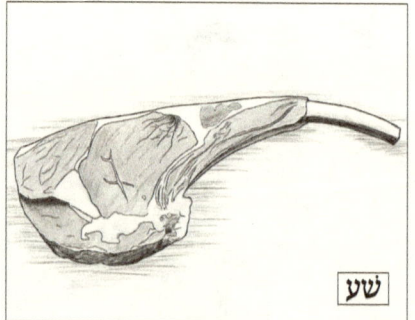 

בָּשָׂר   לֶחֶם

כָּל־בָּשָׂר אֲשֶׁר־בּוֹ רוּחַ חַיִּים   וּבְכָל־אֶרֶץ מִצְרַיִם הָיָה לָחֶם

---

mishté
N: feast, drinking (m)
He made them a feast, and they ate and drank. (Gen 26:30)

ra'áv
N: famine, hunger (m)
There was a famine in the land, and he went down to Egypt. (Gen 12:10)

léxem
N: bread (m)
But in all the land of Egypt there was bread. (Gen 41:54)

basár
N: meat, flesh (m)
"... all flesh in which there is a spirit of life." (Gen 6:17)

 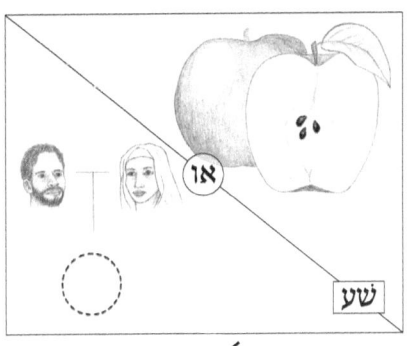

פְּרִי   זֶרַע

וּבֵרַךְ פְּרִי־בִטְנְךָ וּפְרִי־אַדְמָתֶךָ   תֶּן־זֶרַע וְנִחְיֶה וְלֹא נָמוּת

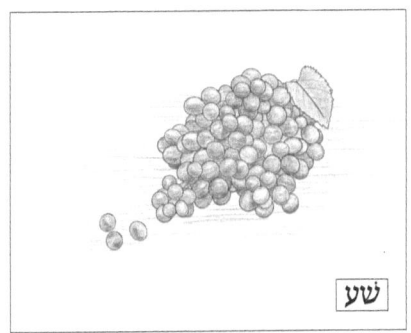 

עֵנָב \ עֲנָבִים   יַיִן

וַיִּכְרְתוּ מִשָּׁם אֶשְׁכּוֹל עֲנָבִים   וּמַלְכִּי־צֶדֶק הוֹצִיא לֶחֶם וָיָיִן

---

prí
N: fruit; offspring (m)
"He will bless the fruit of your womb and of your ground." (Deut 7:13)

zéra
N: seed; offspring (m)
"Give (us) seed, that we might live and not die." (Gen 47:19)

enáv / anavím
N: grape (m)
And they cut from there a cluster of grapes. (Num 13:23)

yáyn
N: wine (m)
And Melchizedek brought out bread and wine. (Gen 14:18)

2.3
Clothing

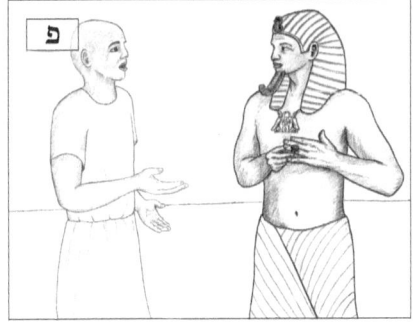

הֵסִיר \ יָסִיר

פַּרְעֹה מֵסִיר טַבַּעְתּוֹ מֵעַל יָדוֹ

סור | וַיָּסַר | הָסֵר | הָסִיר

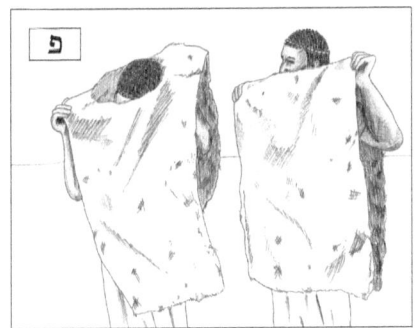

לָבַשׁ \ יִלְבַּשׁ

אַנְשֵׁי נִינְוֵה לֹבְשִׁים שַׂקִּים

לבש | וַיִּלְבַּשׁ | לְבַשׁ | לָבֹשׁ

גִּלָּה \ יְגַלֶּה

רוּת מְגַלָּה אֶת־מַרְגְּלֹת בֹּעַז

גלה | וַיְגַל | גַּל | גַּלּוֹת

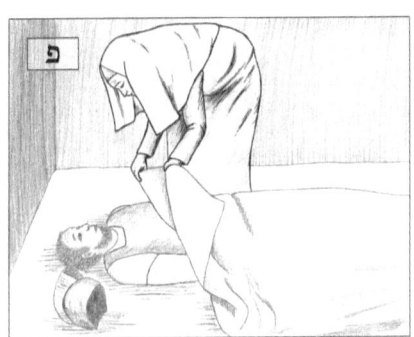

כִּסָּה \ יְכַסֶּה

יָעֵל מְכַסָּה אֶת־סִיסְרָא בַּשְּׂמִיכָה

כסה | וַיְכַס | כַּסֵּה | כַּסּוֹת

---

hesír / yasír
HI: remove
Pharaoh is removing his ring from his hand. (Gen 41:42)

laváš / yilbáš
Q: put on, wear
The men of Nineveh are putting on sackcloth. (Jon 3:5)

gilá / yəgalé
PI: uncover
Ruth is uncovering the place of Boaz's feet. (Ruth 3:7)

kisá / yəxasé
PI: cover
Jael is covering Sisera with the rug. (Judg 4:18)

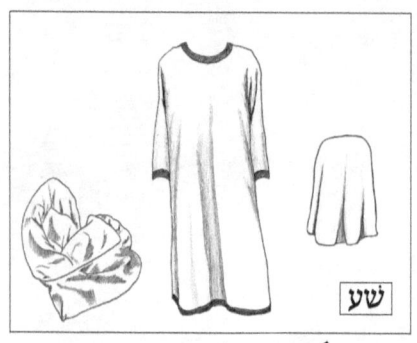

בֶּגֶד \ בְּגָדִים   אֵפוֹד

וַתִּקַּח רִבְקָה אֶת־בִּגְדֵי עֵשָׂו בְּנָהּ   וַיַּעַשׂ אֶת־הָאֵפֹד זָהָב וְאַרְגָּמָן

שִׂמְלָה \ שְׂמָלוֹת   מְעִיל \ מְעִילִים

וַיִּקְרַע יַעֲקֹב שִׂמְלֹתָיו   הִלְבִּישַׁנִי מְעִיל צְדָקָה

---

béged / bəgadím
N: clothes, cloth (m)
And Rebekah took the clothes of
Esau her son. (Gen 27:15)

efód
N: ephod (m)
And he made the ephod out of gold
and of purple wool. (Exod 39:2)

simlá / smalót
N: outer garment (f)
And Jacob tore his garments.
(Gen 37:34)

mə'íl / mə'ilím
N: robe, coat (m)
"He has clothed me with a robe of
righteousness." (Isa 61:10)

Clothing 55

עֲטָרָה \ עֲטָרוֹת
וַיִּקַּח אֶת־עֲטֶרֶת־מַלְכָּם

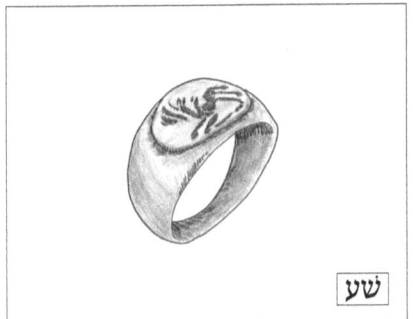

טַבַּעַת \ טַבָּעוֹת
וַיָּסַר הַמֶּלֶךְ אֶת־טַבַּעְתּוֹ מֵעַל יָדוֹ

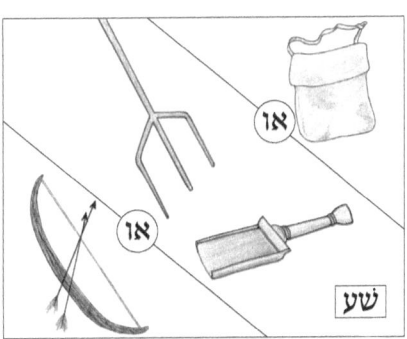

כְּלִי \ כֵּלִים
וַיִּשְׁלַח דָּוִד אֶת־יָדוֹ אֶל־הַכְּלִי

נַעַל \ נְעָלִים
שַׁל־נְעָלֶיךָ מֵעַל רַגְלֶיךָ

---

atará / atarót
N: garland, crown (f)
And he took the crown of their king.
(2 Sam 12:30)

tabá'at / taba'ót
N: ring, signet ring (f)
And the king removed his ring from his hand. (Esth 3:10)

klí / kelím
N: vessel; implement; weapon (m)
And David reached out his hand into the bag. (1 Sam 17:49)

ná'al / na'aláym
N: sandal (f)
"Loosen your sandals from upon your feet." (Exod 3:5)

3
The Social Order

3.1
Family and Tribe

Family and Tribe 59

יָלַד \ יֵלֵד

שָׂרָה יָלְדָה לְאַבְרָהָם בֵּן

ילד | וַיֵּלֶד | — | לֶדֶת

הִרְבָּה \ יַרְבֶּה

יְהוָה מַרְבֶּה אֶת־זֶרַע אַבְרָהָם

רבה | וַיֶּרֶב | הֶרֶב\הִרְבֵּה | הַרְבּוֹת

הוֹלִיד \ יוֹלִיד

אַבְרָהָם מוֹלִיד אֶת־יִצְחָק

ילד | וַיּוֹלֶד | הוֹלֵד | הוֹלִיד

גָּאַל \ יִגְאַל

בֹּעַז גָּאַל אֶת־הַשָּׂדֶה וְאֶת־רוּת

גאל | וַיִּגְאַל | גָּאַל | גְּאֹל

yalád / yeléd
Q: give birth
Sarah gives birth to a son for Abraham. (Gen 21:2)

hirbá / yarbé
HI: make many, multiply
YHWH multiplies the offspring of Abraham. (Gen 26:4)

holíd / yolíd
HI: beget
Abraham begets Isaac. (Gen 25:19)

ga'ál / yig'ál
Q: redeem, buy back
Boaz is redeeming the field and Ruth. (Ruth 4:6)

דּוֹר \ דּוֹרוֹת

וַיָּמָת יוֹסֵף וְכֹל הַדּוֹר הַהוּא

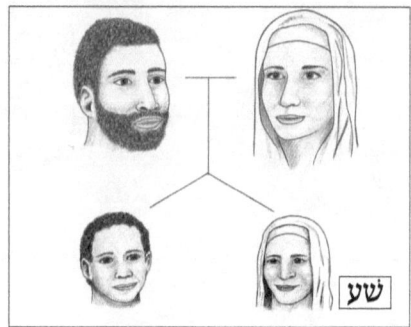

מִשְׁפָּחָה \ מִשְׁפָּחוֹת

וְנִבְרְכוּ בְךָ כֹּל מִשְׁפְּחֹת הָאֲדָמָה

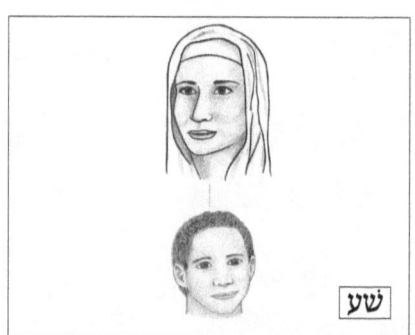

אֵם \ אִמּוֹת

יַעֲזֹב אִישׁ אֶת־אָבִיו וְאֶת־אִמּוֹ

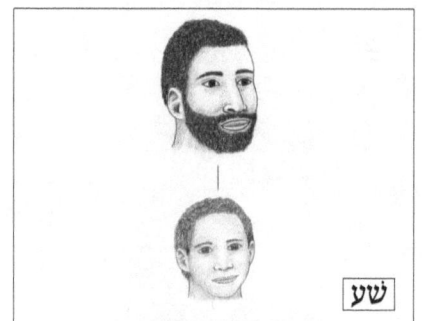

אָב \ אָבוֹת

וְחָם הוּא אֲבִי כְנָעַן

---

dór / dorót
N: generation (m)
Joseph died, and all of that generation. (Exod 1:6)

mishpaxá / mishpaxót
N: family, clan (f)
"And in you will be blessed all the families of the ground." (Gen 12:3)

ém / imót
N: mother (f)
A man shall leave his father and his mother. (Gen 2:24)

áv / avót
N: father (m)
And Ham was the father of Canaan. (Gen 9:18)

בֵּן \ בָּנִים

וַיֵּדַע אָדָם אֶת־אִשְׁתּוֹ וַתֵּלֶד בֵּן

בַּת \ בָּנוֹת

קַח אֶת־אִשְׁתְּךָ וְאֶת־שְׁתֵּי בְנֹתֶיךָ

אָח \ אַחִים

וַיֹּאמֶר קַיִן אֶל־הֶבֶל אָחִיו

אָחוֹת \ אֲחָיוֹת

לָמָה אָמַרְתָּ אֲחֹתִי הִיא

---

bén / baním
N: son (m)
Adam knew his wife, and she bore a son. (Gen 4:25)

bát / banót
N: daughter (f)
"Take your wife and your two daughters." (Gen 19:15)

áx / axím
N: brother (m)
And Cain said to Abel his brother ... (Gen 4:8)

axót / axayót
N: sister (f)
"Why did you say, 'She is my sister'?" (Gen 12:19)

The Social Order

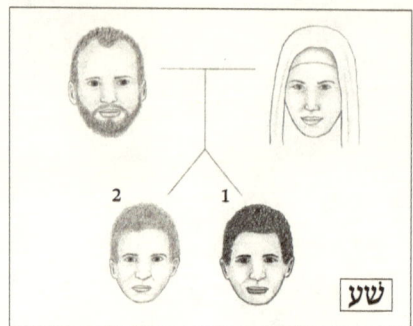

נַחֲלָה \ נְחָלוֹת
נַחֲלָתוֹ הִיא לְבָנָיו תִּהְיֶה

בְּכוֹר \ בְּכוֹרִים
וַיֹּאמֶר אֲנִי בִּנְךָ בְכֹרְךָ עֵשָׂו

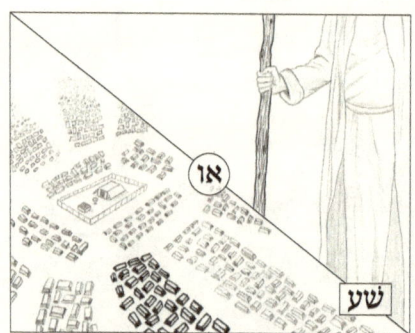

מַטֶּה \ מַטּוֹת
וְאֶת־הַמַּטֶּה הַזֶּה תִּקַּח בְּיָדְךָ

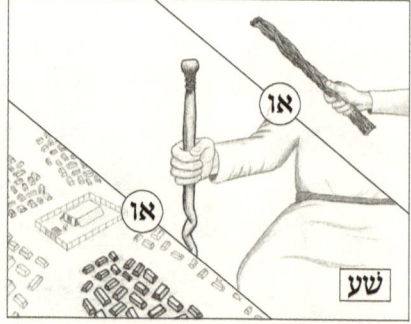

שֵׁבֶט \ שְׁבָטִים
בַּשֵּׁבֶט תַּכֶּנּוּ וְנַפְשׁוֹ תַּצִּיל

---

bəxór / bəxorím
N: firstborn (m)
And he said, "I am your son, your firstborn, Esau." (Gen 27:32)

naxalá / nəxalót
N: inheritance (f)
"It is his inheritance. It shall belong to his sons." (Ezek 46:16)

maté / matót
N: staff; tribe (m)
"And this staff you shall take in your hand." (Exod 4:17)

shévet / shvatím
N: rod, scepter; tribe (m)
With the rod you shall strike him, and his soul you shall rescue. (Prov 23:14)

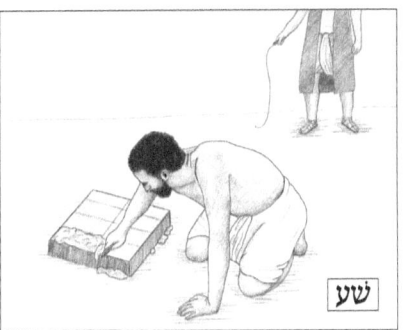 

עֶ֫בֶד \ עֲבָדִים   אָדוֹן \ אֲדֹנִים

עֲבָדִים הָיִינוּ לְפַרְעֹה בְּמִצְרַיִם   וַיִּקַּח הָעֶ֫בֶד עֲשָׂרָה גְמַלֵּי אֲדֹנָיו

רֵעַ \ רֵעִים   נָשִׂיא \ נְשִׂיאִים

לֹא תַחְמֹד בֵּית רֵעֶ֫ךָ   וְנָשִׂיא לִבְנֵי יְהוּדָה נַחְשׁוֹן

adón / adoním
N: lord, master (m)
And the servant took ten of his master's camels. (Gen 24:10)

éved / avadím
N: slave, servant (m)
"Slaves we were to Pharaoh in Egypt." (Deut 6:21)

nasí / nəsi'ím
N: leader, prince (m)
And the leader for the children of Judah was Nahshon. (Num 2:3)

réa / re'ím
N: neighbor, friend (m)
"You shall not desire the house of your neighbor." (Exod 20:17)

# 3.2
Personal Interactions

Personal Interactions

שָׁאַל \ יִשְׁאַל

הָעָם שֹׁאֲלִים מִשְּׁמוּאֵל מֶלֶךְ

שאל | וַיִּשְׁאַל | שָׁאַל | שְׁאַל

עָנָה \ יַעֲנֶה

אֶסְתֵּר עָנָה אֶת־הַמֶּלֶךְ

ענה | וַיַּעַן | עֲנֵה | עֲנוֹת

בִּקֵּשׁ \ יְבַקֵּשׁ

שָׁאוּל מְבַקֵּשׁ אֶת־דָּוִד

בקש | וַיְבַקֵּשׁ | בַּקֵּשׁ | בַּקֵּשׁ

מָצָא \ יִמְצָא

הַכֹּהֵן מֹצֵא אֶת־סֵפֶר הַתּוֹרָה

מצא | וַיִּמְצָא | מְצָא | מְצֹא

---

sha'ál / yish'ál
Q: ask
The people are asking for a king from Samuel. (1 Sam 8:10)

aná / ya'ané
Q: answer
Esther is answering the king. (Esth 5:7)

biqésh / yəvaqésh
PI: seek, look for
Saul is looking for David. (1 Sam 23:14)

matsá / yimtsá
Q: find
The priest finds the Book of the Law. (2 Kgs 22:8)

 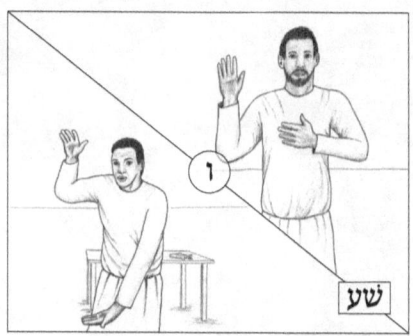

קוֹל \ קוֹלוֹת   אֱמֶת · שֶׁקֶר

וַיֹּאמֶר הַקֹּל קוֹל יַעֲקֹב   אֱמֶת לֹא יְדַבֵּרוּ לִמְּדוּ לְשׁוֹנָם שֶׁקֶר

שָׁלוֹם \ שְׁלוֹמִים   חֵמָה

שָׁלוֹם לְךָ אַל־תִּירָא לֹא תָּמוּת   פִּינְחָס הֵשִׁיב חֲמָתִי מֵעַל יִשְׂרָאֵל

---

qól / qolót
N: voice, noise (m)
And he said, "The voice is the voice of Jacob." (Gen 27:22)

emét / shéqer
N: truth, faithfulness; lie
"Truth they do not speak; they have taught their tongue a lie." (Jer 9:4*)

shalóm / shlomím
N: peace (m)
"Peace to you. Do not fear—you will not die." (Judg 6:23)

xemá
N: wrath (f)
"Phinehas caused my wrath to return from upon Israel." (Num 25:11)

הִגִּיד \ יַגִּיד

שִׁמְשׁוֹן מַגִּיד לִדְלִילָה עַל־שְׂעָרוֹ

נגד | וַיַּגֵּד | הַגֵּד | הִגִּיד

סִפֵּר \ יְסַפֵּר

יוֹסֵף מְסַפֵּר חֲלוֹם לְאֶחָיו

ספר | וַיְסַפֵּר | סַפֵּר | סַפֵּר

נִבָּא \ יִנָּבֵא

יִרְמְיָהוּ נִבָּא בַּחֲצַר בֵּית־יְהוָה

נבא | וַיִּנָּבֵא | הִנָּבֵא | הִנָּבֵא

נִשְׁבַּע \ יִשָּׁבַע

עֵשָׂו נִשְׁבַּע לְמִכְרוֹ בְּכֹרָתוֹ לְיַעֲקֹב

שבע | וַיִּשָּׁבַע | הִשָּׁבַע | הִשָּׁבַע

---

higíd / yagíd
HI: tell, inform
Samson is telling Delilah about his hair. (Judg 16:17)

sipér / yəsapér
PI: recount, give the details
Joseph is recounting a dream for his brothers. (Gen 37:9)

nibá / yinavé
NI: prophesy
Jeremiah is prophesying in the court of YHWH's house. (Jer 19:14)

nishbá / yishavá
NI: swear
Esau is swearing to sell his birthright to Jacob. (Gen 25:33)

The Social Order

קָהָל

וַיַּקְהִ֜לוּ מֹשֶׁ֧ה וְאַהֲרֹ֛ן אֶת־הַקָּהָ֖ל

עֵדָה

וְלֹא־הָ֥יָה מַ֖יִם לָעֵדָ֑ה

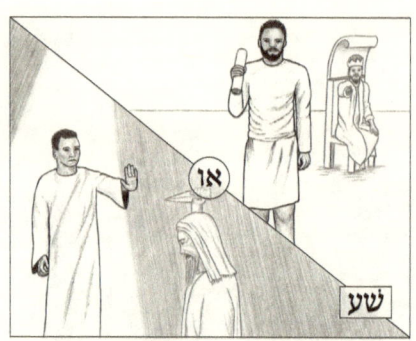

מַלְאָךְ \ מַלְאָכִים

וַיִּשְׁלַ֥ח שָׁא֛וּל מַלְאָכִ֖ים אֶל־יִשָׁ֑י

נְאֻם

וְקַמְתִּ֣י עֲלֵיהֶ֔ם נְאֻם־יְהוָ֖ה

---

qahál
N: assembly (m)
Moses and Aaron assembled the assembly. (Num 20:10)

edáh
N: congregation (f)
But there was no water for the congregation. (Num 20:2)

mal'áx / mal'axím
N: messenger; angel (m)
And Saul sent messengers to Jesse. (1 Sam 16:19)

nə'úm
N: declaration
"And I will rise up against them," the declaration of YHWH. (Isa 14:22)

Personal Interactions

לִקְרַאת | פָּקַד \ יִפְקֹד

*יוֹסֵף עָלָה לִקְרַאת יִשְׂרָאֵל אָבִיו

דָּוִד פָּקַד אֶת־אֶחָיו לְשָׁלוֹם

פקד | וַיִּפְקֹד | פָּקֹד | פְּקֹד

קרא | 95% of this root's instances are in the above infinitive form

נָטָה \ יִטֶּה | שָׁלַח \ יִשְׁלַח

בַּת־פַּרְעֹה שָׁלְחָה אֶת־אֲמָתָהּ

מֹשֶׁה נָטָה אֶת־יָדוֹ עַל־הַיָּם

שלח | וַיִּשְׁלַח | שָׁלַח | שְׁלַח

נטה | וַיֵּט | נָטָה | נְטוֹת

---

paqád / yifqód
Q: visit; list, look after; appoint
David is visiting his brothers to see if they are well. (1 Sam 17:18)

liqrát
Q: meet, encounter
Joseph is going up to meet Israel his father. (Gen 46:29)

shaláx / yishláx
Q: send
The daughter of Pharaoh is sending her servant girl. (Exod 2:5)

natá / yité
Q: stretch out; turn
Moses is stretching out his hand upon the sea. (Exod 14:21)

3.3
Worship/Cultic

Worship/Cultic

טוֹב \ טוֹבָה

וַיַּרְא אֱלֹהִים וְהִנֵּה־טוֹב מְאֹד

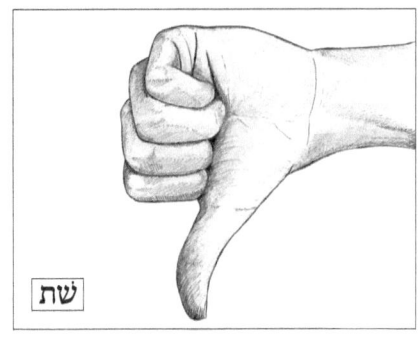

רַע \ רָעָה

הָיָה כְּאַחַד מִמֶּנּוּ לָדַעַת טוֹב וָרָע

צַדִּיק \ צַדִּיקָה

נֹחַ אִישׁ צַדִּיק

רָשָׁע \ רִשְׁעָה

הַאַף תִּסְפֶּה צַדִּיק עִם־רָשָׁע

---

tóv / tová
ADJ: good (m/f)
God saw and, behold, it was very good. (Gen 1:31)

tsadíq / tsadiqá
ADJ: righteous, just (m/f)
Noah was a righteous man. (Gen 6:9)

rá / ra'á
ADJ: bad, evil (m/f)
"He has become like one of us, knowing good and evil." (Gen 3:22)

rashá / rəsha'á
ADJ: guilty, wicked (m/f)
"Will you indeed sweep away righteous with wicked?" (Gen 18:23)

תּוֹעֵבָה \ תּוֹעֵבוֹת
יַעֲשֶׂה פֶסֶל תּוֹעֲבַת יְהוָה

חַטָּאת \ חַטֹּאת
אֲכַפְּרָה בְּעַד חַטַּאתְכֶם

עָוֹן \ עֲוֹנוֹת
שָׁבוּ עַל־עֲוֹנֹת אֲבוֹתָם הָרִאשֹׁנִים

בַּעַל \ בְּעָלִים
וּבַעַל הַשּׁוֹר נָקִי

---

to'evá / to'evót
N: abomination (f)
"He makes an idol, an abomination to Yahweh." (Deut 27:15)

xatát / xatót
N: sin; sin offering (f)
"I shall atone for your sin." (Exod 32:30)

avón / avonót
N: transgression, iniquity (m)
"They have returned to the iniquities of their first fathers." (Jer 11:10)

bá'al / bə'alím
N: owner, husband; Baal (m)
"But the owner of the ox is innocent." (Exod 21:28)

Worship/Cultic

חָטָא \ יֶחֱטָא   הֵרַע \ יָרַע

עָכָן חֹטֵא לַיהוָה   הָעֹשֶׂה פֶּסֶל מֵרַע

חטא | וַיֶּחֱטָא | — | חָטָא   רעע | וַיָּרַע | — | הֵרַע

טָמֵא \ יִטְמָא   חִלֵּל \ יְחַלֵּל

הַחֲזִיר טָמֵא לַבָּנִים אֲשֶׁר לַיהוָה   הַנֹּתֵן לַמֹּלֶךְ מְחַלֵּל אֶת־שֵׁם יְהוָה

טמא | וַיִּטְמָא | — | טָמְאָה   חלל | וַיְחַלֵּל | — | חִלֵּל

xatá / yexetá
Q: sin
Achan is sinning against YHWH. (Josh 7:20)

herá / yará
HI: do evil
The one who makes an idol does an evil thing. (1 Kgs 14:9)

tamé / yitmá
Q: be unclean
The pig is unclean for the children that belong to YHWH. (Deut 14:8)

xilél / yəxalél
PI: profane
The one who gives to Molech profanes YHWH's name. (Lev 20:3)

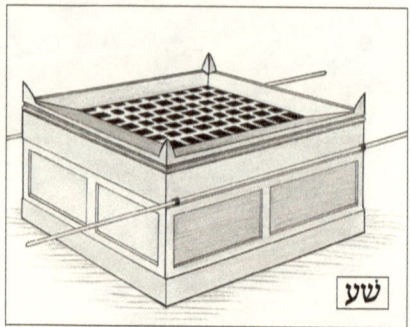

מִזְבֵּחַ \ מִזְבְּחוֹת

וַיִּבֶן שָׁם אַבְרָהָם אֶת־הַמִּזְבֵּחַ

זֶבַח \ זְבָחִים

וְאֶת־הָאַיִל יַעֲשֶׂה זֶבַח שְׁלָמִים

מִנְחָה \ מְנָחוֹת

מִנְחָה הִיא שְׁלוּחָה לַאדֹנִי לְעֵשָׂו

עֹלָה \ עֹלוֹת

וְכֶבֶשׂ בֶּן־שְׁנָתוֹ תַּעֲשֶׂה עֹלָה

---

mizbéax / mizbəxót
N: altar (m)
And there Abraham built the altar.
(Gen 22:9)

zévax / zvaxím
N: sacrifice (m)
"And the ram he shall make as a sacrifice of peace." (Num 6:17)

minxá / minxót
N: gift, offering (f)
"It is a gift sent to my lord, to Esau."
(Gen 32:19*)

olá / olót
N: whole burnt offering (f)
"A year-old sheep you shall make as a whole burnt offering." (Ezek 46:13)

Worship/Cultic

כִּפֶּר \ יְכַפֵּר

אַהֲרֹן מְכַפֵּר בַּעֲדוֹ וּבְעַד הָעָם

כפר | וַיְכַפֵּר | כִּפֵּר | כַּפֵּר

זָבַח \ יִזְבַּח

הַמַּלָּחִים זֹבְחִים זֶבַח לַיהוָה

זבח | וַיִּזְבַּח | זָבַח | זֶבַח

הִקְטִיר \ יַקְטִיר

אַהֲרֹן מַקְטִיר קְטֹרֶת סַמִּים

קטר | וַיַּקְטֵר | הַקְטֵר | הַקְטִיר

שָׂרַף \ יִשְׂרֹף

מֹשֶׁה שָׂרַף אֶת־הָעֵגֶל בָּאֵשׁ

שרף | וַיִּשְׂרֹף | שְׂרֹף | שָׂרֹף

---

zaváx / yizbáx
Q: slaughter, sacrifice
The sailors are sacrificing a sacrifice to YHWH. (Jon 1:16)

kipér / yəxapér
PI: atone, cover
Aaron is atoning for himself and for the people. (Lev 16:24)

saráf / yisróf
Q: burn
Moses is burning the calf with fire. (Exod 32:20)

hiqtír / yaqtír
HI: make smoke (incense/sacrifice)
Aaron is burning an incense of spices. (Exod 30:7)

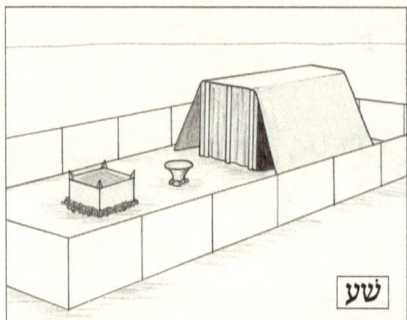
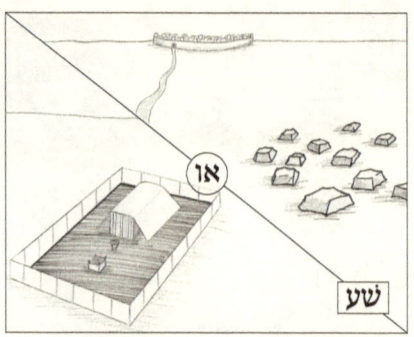

מִשְׁכָּן \ מִשְׁכָּנוֹת   חָצֵר \ חֲצֵרוֹת

וַיָּבֵא אֶת־הָאָרֹן אֶל־הַמִּשְׁכָּן   עָרִים שְׁתַּיִם וְחַצְרֵיהֶן

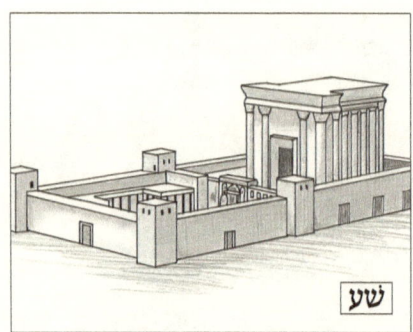

הֵיכָל \ הֵיכָלוֹת   עַמּוּד \ עַמּוּדִים

וְהוּא יִבְנֶה אֶת־הֵיכַל יְהוָה   וַיָּקֶם אֶת־הָעַמֻּדִים לְאֻלָם הַהֵיכָל

---

mishkán / mishkanót
N: tabernacle (f)
And he brought the ark into the tabernacle. (Exod 40:21)

xatsér / xatserót
N: village; courtyard (f)
... two cities and their villages. (Josh 15:60)

hexál / hexalót
N: temple; palace (m)
"And he will build the temple of YHWH." (Zech 6:13)

amúd / amudím
N: pillar (m)
And he raised the pillars for the porch of the temple. (1 Kgs 7:21)

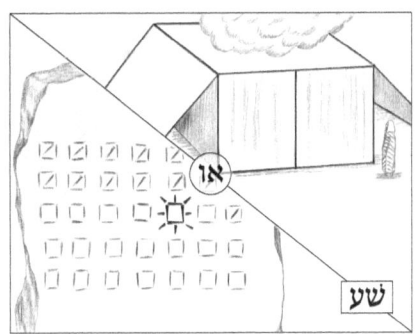

מוֹעֵד \ מוֹעֲדִים
וַיָּשֶׂם אֶת־הַמְּנֹרָה בְּאֹהֶל מוֹעֵד

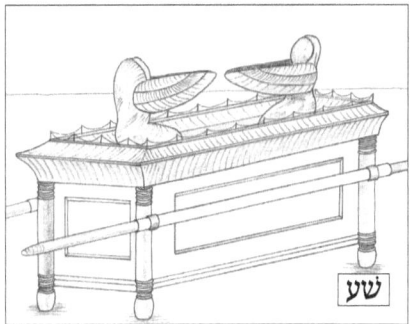

אָרוֹן
וְעָשׂוּ אֲרוֹן עֲצֵי שִׁטִּים

בָּמָה \ בָּמוֹת
וַיִּבְנוּ גַם־הֵמָּה לָהֶם בָּמוֹת

חוּץ \ חוּצוֹת
וַיִּשְׂרְפֵם מִחוּץ לִירוּשָׁלָ͏ִם

---

mo'éd / mo'adím
N: appointed place/time (m)
He placed the lampstand in the tent of meeting. (Exod 40:24)

arón
N: chest, ark (m)
"And they shall make an ark of wood from acacia trees." (Exod 25:10)

bamá / bamót
N: (cultic) high place (f)
And they also built for themselves high places. (1 Kgs 14:23)

xúts / xutsót
N: outside (sg); streets (pl)
And he burned them outside of Jerusalem. (2 Kgs 23:4)

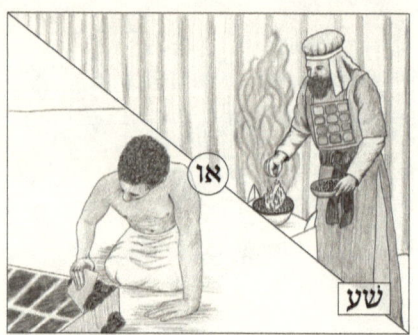

כֹּהֵן \ כֹּהֲנִים   עֲבֹדָה

וְלָקַח הַכֹּהֵן מִדַּם הַפָּר   לַעֲבֹד אֶת־עֲבֹדָתָם בְּאֹהֶל מוֹעֵד

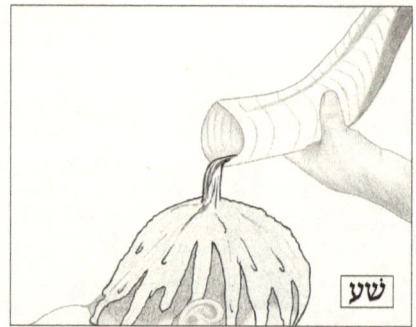

דָּם \ דָּמִים   שֶׁמֶן \ שְׁמָנִים

וַיִּטְבְּלוּ אֶת־הַכֻּתֹּנֶת בַּדָּם   וַיִּקַּח שְׁמוּאֵל אֶת־קֶרֶן הַשֶּׁמֶן

---

kohén / kohaním
N: priest (m)
"The priest shall take from the blood of the bull." (Lev 4:5)

avodá
N: service; work, slavery (f)
... to perform their service in the tent of meeting. (Num 8:22)

dám / damím
N: blood (m)
And they dipped the tunic in the blood. (Gen 37:31)

shémen / shmaním
N: oil (m)
And Samuel took the horn of oil. (1 Sam 16:13)

Worship/Cultic

קָדוֹשׁ \ קְדֹשָׁה

וִהְיִיתֶם לִי קְדֹשִׁים כִּי קָדוֹשׁ אֲנִי

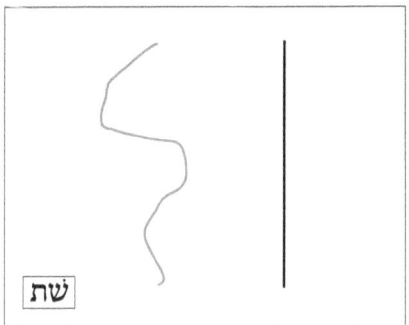

יָשָׁר \ יְשָׁרָה

וַיַּדְרִיכֵם בְּדֶרֶךְ יְשָׁרָה

חָכָם \ חֲכָמָה

הִנֵּה נָתַתִּי לְךָ לֵב חָכָם וְנָבוֹן

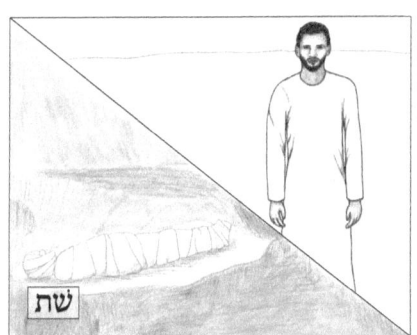

חַי \ חַיָּה

וַיַּגִּדוּ לוֹ לֵאמֹר עוֹד יוֹסֵף חַי

---

yashár / yəshará
ADJ: straight, (up)right (m/f)
"And he made them tread in a straight path." (Ps 107:7)

xáy / xayá
ADJ: alive, living (m/f)
And they told him, saying, "Joseph is still alive." (Gen 45:26)

qadósh / qədoshá
ADJ: holy (m/f)
"You shall be holy to me, because I am holy." (Lev 20:26)

xaxám / xaxamá
ADJ: wise (m/f)
"Behold, I give to you a wise and discerning heart." (1 Kgs 3:12)

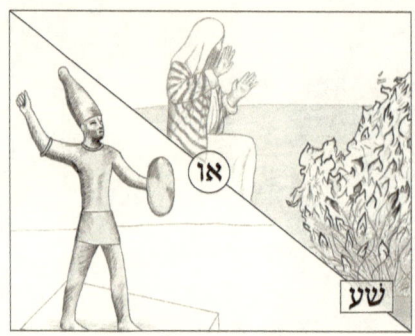

אֵל \ אֱלֹהִים   YHWH

אָנֹכִי אֱלֹהֵי אָבִיךָ אֱלֹהֵי אַבְרָהָם   וַיְדַבֵּר אֱלֹהִים אֶל־מֹשֶׁה אֲנִי יְהוָה

 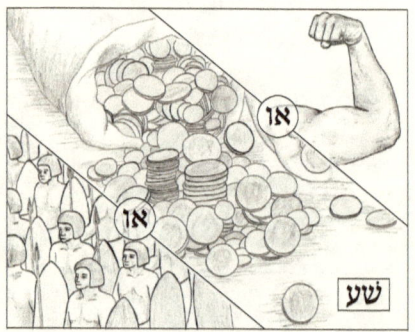

כָּבוֹד   חַיִל

כִּי־מָלֵא הַכָּבוֹד אֶת־בֵּית יְהוָה   וַתָּבֹא יְרוּשָׁלַמָה בְּחַיִל כָּבֵד מְאֹד

él / elohím
N: God; god (m)
"I am the God of your father, the God of Abraham." (Exod 3:6)

adonáy
N: (God's covenant name) (m)
And God said to Moses, "I am YHWH." (Exod 6:2)

kavód
N: glory (m)
... because the glory filled the house of YHWH. (1 Kgs 8:11)

xáyl
N: strength; wealth; army (m)
And she came to Jerusalem with very much wealth. (1 Kgs 10:2)

Worship/Cultic 81

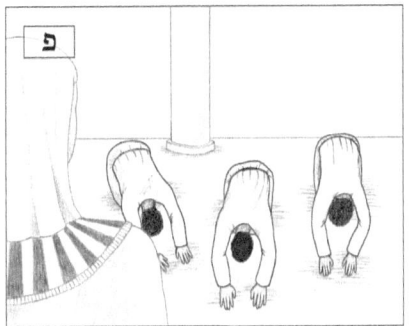

הִשְׁתַּחֲוָה \ יִשְׁתַּחֲוֶה

אֲחֵי יוֹסֵף מִשְׁתַּחֲוִים לוֹ

חוה | וַיִּשְׁתַּ֫חוּ | הִשְׁתַּחֲוָה | הִשְׁתַּחֲוֹת

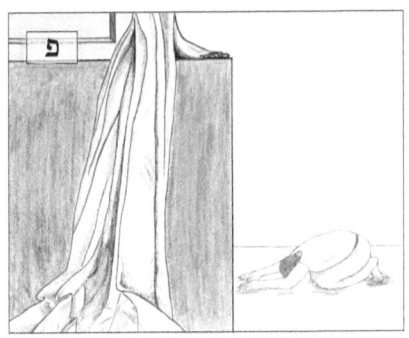

רָם \ יָרוּם

רָם אֲדֹנָי אֲשֶׁר עַל־כִּסֵּא

רום | וַיָּ֫רָם | רוּם | רום

הִלֵּל \ יְהַלֵּל

דָּוִד מְהַלֵּל אֶת־יְהוָה בְּתוֹךְ קָהָל

הלל | וַיְהַלֵּל | הַלֵּל | הַלֵּל

הוֹדָה \ יוֹדֶה

לֵאָה מוֹדָה אֶת־יְהוָה עַל־יְהוּדָה

ידה | — | הוֹדָה | הוֹדוֹת

---

rám / yarúm
Q: be high, be exalted
Adonai is high who is on a throne.
(Isa 6:1)

hishtaxavá / yishtaxavé
HSTFL: bow down
Joseph's brothers are bowing down to him. (Gen 42:6)

hodá / yodé
HI: thank, praise
Leah is thanking YHWH for Judah.
(Gen 29:35)

hilél / yəhalél
PI: praise
David is praising YHWH in the midst of an assembly. (Ps 22:23*)

3.4
People, Law, and Covenant

People, Law, and Covenant 83

מַמְלָכָה \ מַמְלָכוֹת
לֹא־אֶקַּח אֶת־כָּל־הַמַּמְלָכָה מִיָּדוֹ

מֶ֫לֶךְ \ מְלָכִים
בֹּא דַבֵּר אֶל־פַּרְעֹה מֶ֫לֶךְ מִצְרָיִם

עַם \ עַמִּים
עַם בְּנֵי יִשְׂרָאֵל רַב וְעָצוּם מִמֶּ֫נּוּ

גּוֹי \ גּוֹיִם
תִּהְיוּ מַמְלֶ֫כֶת כֹּהֲנִים וְגוֹי קָדוֹשׁ

---

mamlaxá / mamlaxót
N: kingdom (f)
"I will not take all of the kingdom from his hand." (1 Kgs 11:34)

mélex / mlaxím
N: king (m)
"Enter, speak to Phraoh, the king of Egypt." (Exod 6:11)

ám / amím
N: people (m)
"The people of the Israelites are too many and strong for us." (Exod 1:9)

góy / goyím
N: nation (m)
"You shall be a kingdom of priests and a holy nation." (Exod 19:6)

חֹק · חֻקָּה   מִצְוָה \ מִצְוֹת

וּשְׁמַרְתֶּם אֶת־הַמַּצּוֹת חֻקַּת עוֹלָם   מִצְוֹתָיו אֲשֶׁר־צִוָּה אֶת־מֹשֶׁה

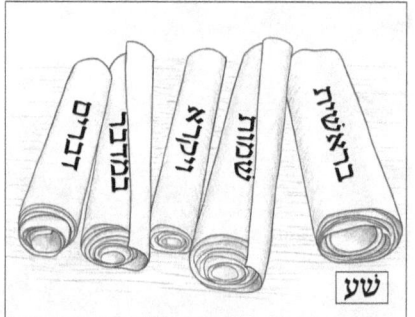

מִשְׁפָּט \ מִשְׁפָּטִים   תּוֹרָה \ תּוֹרוֹת

וְשָׁאַל לוֹ בְּמִשְׁפַּט הָאוּרִים   כַּכָּתוּב בְּתוֹרַת מֹשֶׁה

xóq / xuqá
N: statute, prescription (m/f)
"You shall keep the Unleavened Bread as a statute forever." (Exod 12:17)

mitsvá / mitsvót
N: commandment (f)
"... his commandments that he commanded Moses." (2 Kgs 18:6)

mishpát / mishpatím
N: judgment, decision (m)
"And he shall ask for him by the judgment of the Urim." (Num 27:21)

torá / torót
N: law, instruction (f)
"... as it is written in the Law of Moses." (1 Kgs 2:3)

People, Law, and Covenant

צִוָּה \ יְצַוֶּה

מֹשֶׁה מְצַוֶּה אֶת־הָעָם יִשְׂרָאֵל

צוה | וַיְצַו | צַו\צַוֵּה | צִוּוֹת

שָׁמַר \ יִשְׁמֹר

כְּרֻבִים שֹׁמְרִים דֶּרֶךְ עֵץ הַחַיִּים

שמר | וַיִּשְׁמֹר | שְׁמֹר | שָׁמַר

דָּרַשׁ \ יִדְרֹשׁ

שָׁאוּל דֹּרֵשׁ בְּאֵשֶׁת בַּעֲלַת־אוֹב

דרש | וַיִּדְרֹשׁ | דְּרֹשׁ | דָּרַשׁ

שָׁפַט \ יִשְׁפֹּט

שְׁלֹמֹה שֹׁפֵט בֵּין שְׁתַּיִם נָשִׁים

שפט | וַיִּשְׁפֹּט | שְׁפֹט | שָׁפַט

---

shamár / yishmór
Q: guard, keep
Cherubim are guarding the way to the tree of life. (Gen 3:24)

shafát / yishpót
Q: judge
Solomon is judging between two women. (1 Kgs 3:28)

tsivá / yətsavé
PI: command
Moses is commanding the people, Israel. (Deut 4:13)

darásh / yidrósh
Q: inquire, seek
Saul is inquiring of a female necromancer. (1 Sam 28:7)

חֶ֫סֶד \ חֲסָדִים

הַנֶּאֱמָן שֹׁמֵר הַבְּרִית וְהַחֶ֫סֶד

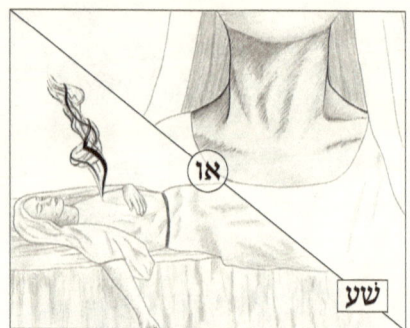

נֶ֫פֶשׁ \ נְפָשׁוֹת

הוֹשִׁיעֵ֫נִי כִּי בָ֫אוּ מַ֫יִם עַד־נָ֫פֶשׁ

בְּרִית

וַיִּכְרְתוּ שְׁנֵיהֶם בְּרִית לִפְנֵי יְהוָה

מְלָאכָה \ מְלָאכוֹת

שֵׁ֫שֶׁת יָמִים תֵּעָשֶׂה מְלָאכָה

xésed / xasadím
N: steadfast love (m)
"... the faithful one keeping the covenant and steadfast love." (Deut 7:9)

brít
N: covenant (f)
And the two of them cut a covenant before YHWH. (1 Sam 23:18)

néfesh / nəfashót
N: throat; soul, living being (f)
"Save me, because water has come up to (my) throat." (Ps 69:2*)

mlaxá / mal'axót
N: work, occupation (f)
"Six days work shall be done." (Exod 35:2)

People, Law, and Covenant 87

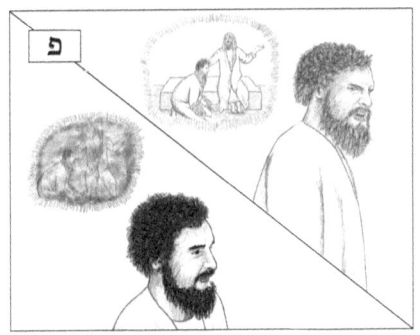

שָׁכַח \ יִשְׁכַּח

עֵשָׂו שָׁכַח אֵת אֲשֶׁר־עָשָׂה יַעֲקֹב

שכח | וַיִּשְׁכַּח | שָׁכַח | שָׁכֹחַ

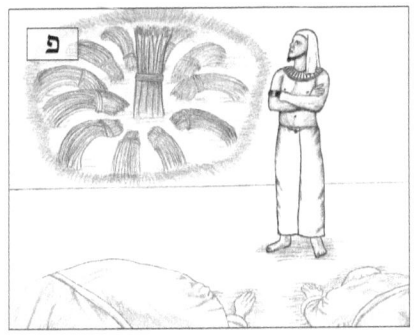

זָכַר \ יִזְכֹּר

יוֹסֵף זָכַר אֶת הַחֲלוֹם

זכר | וַיִּזְכֹּר | זָכַר | זָכֹר

שָׁבַר \ יִשְׁבֹּר

אַנְשֵׁי גִדְעוֹן שֹׁבְרִים כַּדִּים

שבר | וַיִּשְׁבֹּר | שָׁבַר | שָׁבֹר

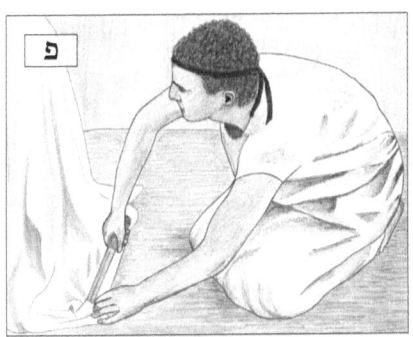

כָּרַת \ יִכְרֹת

דָּוִד כָּרַת אֶת־כְּנַף־מְעִיל שָׁאוּל

כרת | וַיִּכְרֹת | כָּרֹת | כָּרַת

---

shaxáx / yishkáx
Q: forget
Esau forgets what Jacob did.
(Gen 27:45)

zaxár / yizkór
Q: remember
Joseph remembers the dream.
(Gen 42:9)

shavár / yishbór
Q: break
The men of Gideon are breaking pitchers. (Judg 7:20)

karát / yixrót
Q: cut
David is cutting the edge of Saul's robe. (1 Sam 24:5*)

88 The Social Order

בֵּרַךְ \ יְבָרֵךְ

יִצְחָק מְבָרֵךְ אֶת־יַעֲקֹב

ברך | וַיְבָרֶךְ | בָּרֵךְ | בָּרַךְ

קִלֵּל \ יְקַלֵּל

שִׁמְעִי מְקַלֵּל אֶת־דָּוִד

קלל | וַיְקַלֵּל | קַלֵּל | קִלֵּל

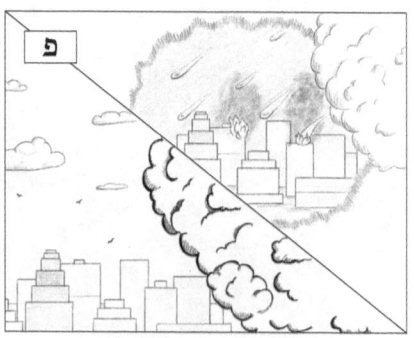

נִחַם \ יִנָּחֵם

הָאֱלֹהִים נִחָם עַל־הָרָעָה לְנִינְוֵה

נחם | וַיִּנָּחֶם | הִנָּחֵם | הִנָּחֵם

שִׁחֵת \ יְשַׁחֵת

אֱלֹהִים מְשַׁחֵת אֶת־סְדֹם

שחת | — | שַׁחֵת | שַׁחֵת

        beráx / yəvaréx
            PI: bless
    Isaac is blessing Jacob.
         (Gen 27:27)

        nixám / yinaxém
  NI: regret, relent; be comforted
God relents concerning the disaster
   against Nineveh. (Jon 3:10)

        qilél / yəqalél
          PI: curse
  Shimei is cursing David.
     (2 Sam 19:22)

       shixét / yəshaxét
     PI: ruin, destroy
  God is destroying Sodom.
      (Gen 19:29)

People, Law, and Covenant 89

הוֹלִיךְ \ יוֹלִיךְ

מֹשֶׁה מוֹלִיךְ אֶת־הָעָם בְּתוֹךְ הַיָּם

הלך | וַיּוֹלֵךְ | הוֹלֵךְ | הוֹלִיךְ

רָעָה \ יִרְעֶה

דָּוִד רֹעֶה אֶת־צֹאן אָבִיו

רעה | וַיִּרְעֶה | רֹעֶה | רְעוֹת

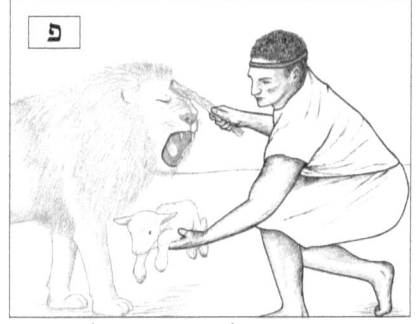

הִצִּיל \ יַצִּיל

דָּוִד מַצִּיל שֶׂה מִפִּי הָאֲרִי

נצל | וַיַּצֵּל | הַצֵּל | הִצִּיל

הוֹשִׁיעַ \ יוֹשִׁיעַ

יְהוָה מוֹשִׁיעַ אֶת־יִשְׂרָאֵל

ישע | וַיּוֹשַׁע | הוֹשַׁע | הוֹשִׁיעַ

holíx / yolíx
HI: lead
Moses is leading the people in the midst of the sea. (Ps 106:9)

ra'á / yir'é
Q: tend; graze
David is shepherding the flock of his father. (1 Sam 17:34)

hitsíl / yatsíl
HI: rescue
David is rescuing a lamb from the mouth of the lion. (1 Sam 17:35)

hoshía / yoshía
HI: help, save
YHWH is saving Israel. (Exod 14:30)

3.5
Lands and Warfare

Lands and Warfare 91

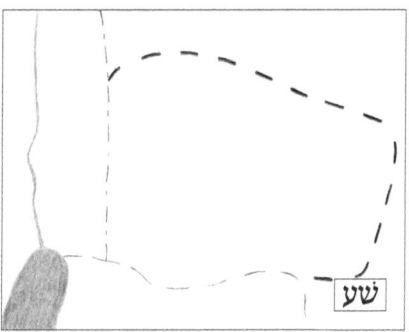

גְּבוּל \ גְּבוּלוֹת
וְזֶה־יִהְיֶה לָכֶם גְּבוּל צָפוֹן

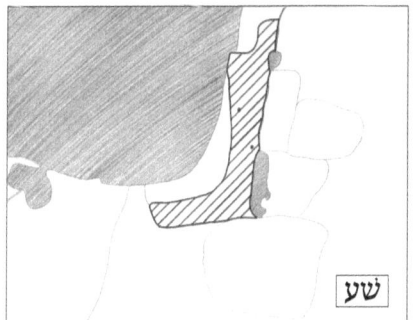

יִשְׂרָאֵל
וַיִּתֵּן לְיִשְׂרָאֵל אֶת־כָּל־הָאָרֶץ

יְרוּשָׁלַםִ
שָׁלֹשׁ שָׁנִים מָלַךְ בִּירוּשָׁלָםִ

שֹׁמְרוֹן
מָלַךְ עַל־יִשְׂרָאֵל בְּשֹׁמְרוֹן

---

gvúl / gvulót
N: border (m)
"And this shall be for you a northern border." (Num 34:7)

yisra'él
N: Israel (m)
And he gave to Israel all the land. (Josh 21:43)

yərushaláym
N: Jerusalem (f)
Three years he reigned in Jerusalem. (1 Kgs 15:2)

shomrón
N: Samaria (f)
He reigned over Israel in Samaria. (1 Kgs 22:52*)

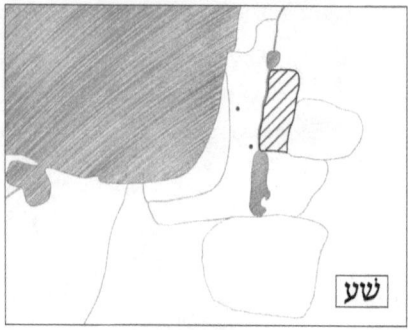

גִּלְעָד
וְאֶרֶץ הַגִּלְעָד הָיְתָה לִבְנֵי־מְנַשֶּׁה

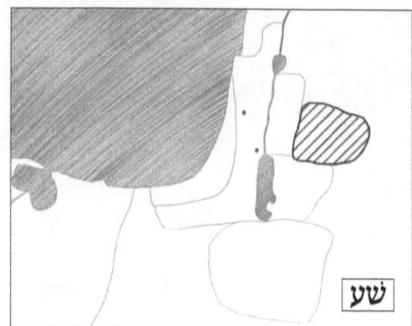

עַמּוֹן
וַיַּעַבְרוּ בְנֵי־עַמּוֹן אֶת־הַיַּרְדֵּן

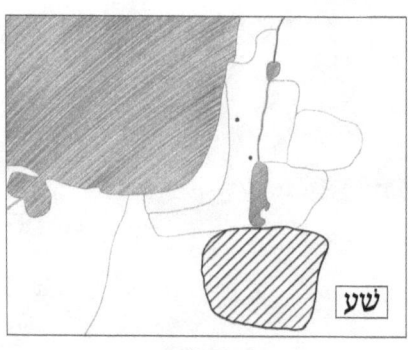

אֱדוֹם
וַיְמָאֵן אֱדוֹם נְתֹן אֶת־יִשְׂרָאֵל עֲבֹר

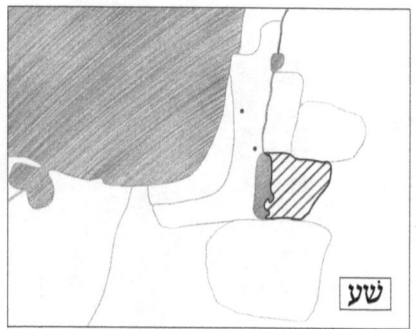

מוֹאָב
וַיֵּלֶךְ אִישׁ לָגוּר בִּשְׂדֵי מוֹאָב

---

gil'ád
N: Gilead
And the land of Gilead belonged to the children of Manasseh. (Josh 17:6)

amón
N: Ammon
And the children of Ammon crossed over the Jordan. (Judg 10:9)

edóm
N: Edom
And Edom refused to allow Israel to pass by. (Num 20:21)

mo'áv
N: Moab
A man went to dwell in the fields of Moab. (Ruth 1:1)

Lands and Warfare

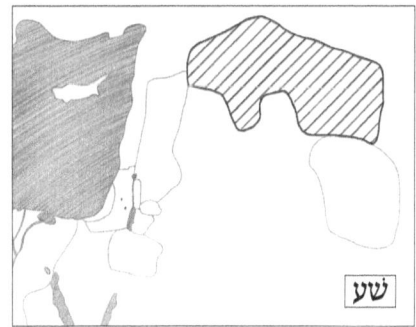

אַשּׁוּר
וַיִּשְׁלַח חִזְקִיָּה אֶל־מֶֽלֶךְ־אַשּׁוּר

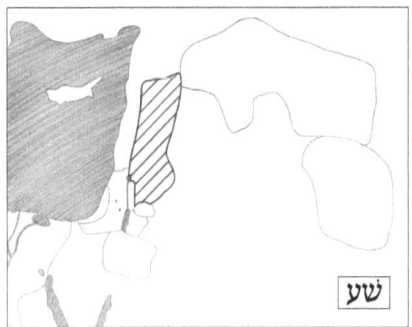

אֲרָם
וַיַּהֲרֹג מֵאֲרָם שְׁבַע מֵאוֹת רֶכֶב

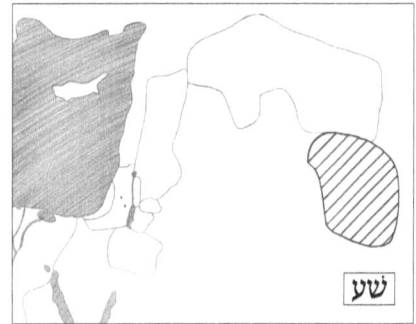

בָּבֶל
וַיָּבֹא מֶֽלֶךְ־בָּבֶל עַל־הָעִיר

מִצְרַיִם
וַיֵּרֶד אַבְרָם מִצְרַיְמָה לָגוּר שָׁם

---

arám
N: Aram
And he slayed from Aram 700 chariots. (2 Sam 10:18)

ashúr
N: Assyria
And Hezekiah sent to the king of Assyria. (2 Kgs 18:14)

mitsráym
N: Egypt
And Abram went down to Egypt to dwell there. (Gen 12:10)

bavél
N: Babylon (Babel)
And the king of Babylon came against the city. (2 Kgs 24:11)

מִלְחָמָה \ מִלְחָמוֹת
וַיֵּצֵא לִקְרַאת פְּלִשְׁתִּים לַמִּלְחָמָה

מַחֲנֶה \ מַחֲנוֹת
וַתַּעַל הַשְּׂלָו וַתְּכַס אֶת־הַמַּחֲנֶה

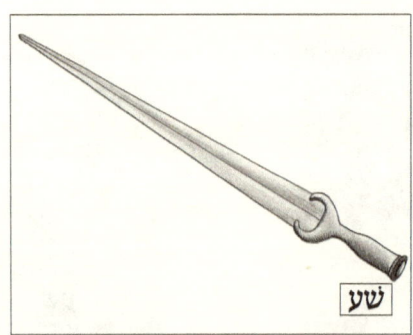

חֶרֶב \ חֲרָבוֹת
וַיַּעַשׂ לוֹ אֵהוּד חֶרֶב

רֶכֶב
וַיָּשֻׁבוּ הַמַּיִם וַיְכַסּוּ אֶת־הָרֶכֶב

---

milxamá / milxamót
N: battle, war (f)
He went out to meet the
Philistines for battle. (1 Sam 4:1)

maxané / maxanót
N: camp (m)
The quail came up and covered the
camp. (Exod 16:13)

xérev / xaravót
N: sword (f)
And Ehud made for himself a sword.
(Judg 3:16)

réxev
N: chariot(s) (m)
The water returned and covered the
chariots. (Exod 14:28)

הָרַג \ יַהֲרֹג

שִׁמְעוֹן וְלֵוִי הֹרְגִים אֶת־חֲמוֹר וּבְנוֹ

הרג | וַיַּהֲרֹג | הָרַג | הָרֹג

נִלְחַם \ יִלָּחֵם

דָּוִד נִלְחָם בְּגָלְיָת

לחם | וַיִּלָּחֶם | הִלָּחֵם | הִלָּחֵם

יָרַשׁ \ יִירַשׁ

בְּנֵי־יִשְׂרָאֵל יֹרְשִׁים אֶת־כְּנָעַן

ירש | וַיִּירַשׁ | רֵשׁ | רֶשֶׁת

הִכָּה \ יַכֶּה

מֹשֶׁה מַכֶּה בַּצּוּר

נכה | וַיַּךְ | הַדְ\הַכֵּה | הַכּוֹת

---

harág / yaharóg
Q: slay (usually with a sword)
Simeon and Levi are slaying Hamor
and his son. (Gen 34:26)

yarásh / yirásh
Q: take possession of
The children of Israel are taking
possession of Canaan. (Josh 12:1)

nilxám / yilaxém
NI: fight
David is fighting Goliath.
(1 Sam 17:10)

hiká / yaké
HI: hit, strike
Moses is striking the rock.
(Exod 17:6)

The Social Order

צָבָא \ צְבָאוֹת

וְנַעֲמָן שַׂר־צְבָא מֶלֶךְ־אֲרָם

שַׂר \ שָׂרִים

וַיְשִׂמֵהוּ שַׂר־אֶלֶף

גִּבּוֹר \ גִּבּוֹרִים

וַיִּשְׁלַח אֵת כָּל־הַצָּבָא הַגִּבֹּרִים

אֹיֵב \ אֹיְבִים

צַר וְאוֹיֵב הָמָן הָרָע הַזֶּה

---

tsavá / tsəva'ót
N: army, host (m)
Naaman was the commander of the army of the king of Aram. (2 Kgs 5:1)

sár / sarím
N: commander; chief official (m)
He set him as a commander of a thousand. (1 Sam 18:13)

gibór / giborím
N: warrior, mighty man (m)
And he sent all the army, that is, the mighty men. (2 Sam 10:7)

oyév / oyvím
N: enemy (m)
"A foe and an enemy is this evil Haman." (Esth 7:6)

Lands and Warfare 97

אָבַד \ יֹאבַד

הָאֲתֹנוֹת לַאֲבִי שָׁאוּל אֹבְדוֹת

אבד | וַיֹּאבַד | — | אָבַד

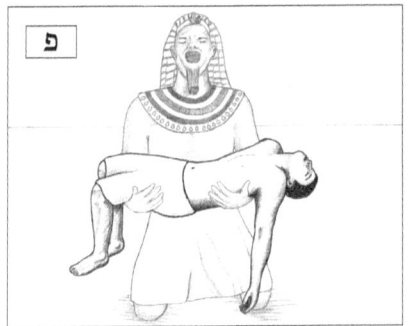

מֵת \ יָמוּת

בְּכוֹר פַּרְעֹה מֵת

מות | וַיָּמָת | מוּת | מֵת

קָבַר \ יִקְבֹּר

בְּנֵי יַעֲקֹב קֹבְרִים אֹתוֹ בִּמְעָרָה

קבר | וַיִּקְבֹּר | קָבֹר | קָבַר

הֵמִית \ יָמִית

דָּוִד מֵמִית אֶת־הָאֲרִי

מות | וַיָּמֶת | הָמֵת | הָמִית

---

avád / yovád
Q: become lost, perish
The donkeys that belong to the father of Saul are lost. (1 Sam 9:3)

qavár / yiqbór
Q: bury
Jacob's sons are burying him in a cave. (Gen 50:13)

mét / yamút
Q: die
The firstborn of Pharaoh is dying. (Exod 11:5)

hemít / yamít
HI: kill
David is killing the lion. (1 Sam 17:35)

3.6
Education

יָדַע \ יֵדַע

נֹחַ יָדַע כִּי־קַלּוּ הַמַּיִם מֵעַל הָאָרֶץ

ידע | וַיֵּדַע | דַּע | דַּעַת

חָשַׁב \ יַחְשֹׁב

עֵלִי חָשַׁב אֶת־חַנָּה לְשִׁכֹּרָה

חשב | וַיַּחְשֹׁב | — | חָשַׁב

הֵבִין \ יָבִין

גַּבְרִיאֵל מֵבִין לוֹ אֶת־הַמַּרְאֶה

בין | וַיָּבֶן | הָבֵן | הָבִין

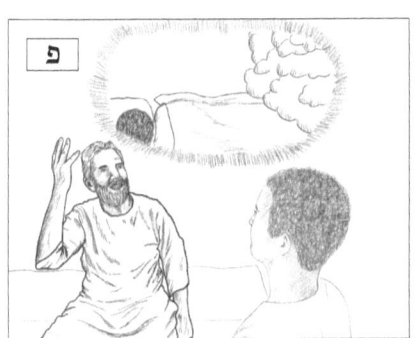

בָּן \ יָבִין

עֵלִי בָּן כִּי יְהוָה קֹרֵא לַנָּעַר

בין | וַיָּבֶן | בִּין | —

---

yadá / yedá
Q: know
Noah knows that the waters became light from upon the earth. (Gen 8:11)

hevín / yavín
HI: explain; understand
Gabriel is explaining to him the vision. (Dan 8:16)

xasháv / yaxshóv
Q: think
Eli thinks Hannah is a drunken woman. (1 Sam 1:13)

bán / yavín
Q: perceive, understand
Eli perceives that YHWH is calling the young man. (1 Sam 3:8)

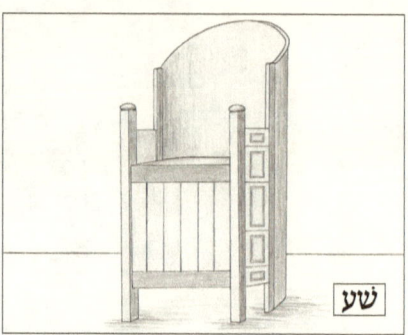

כִּסֵּא \ כִּסְאוֹת

וְנָשִׂים לוֹ שָׁם שֻׁלְחָן וְכִסֵּא

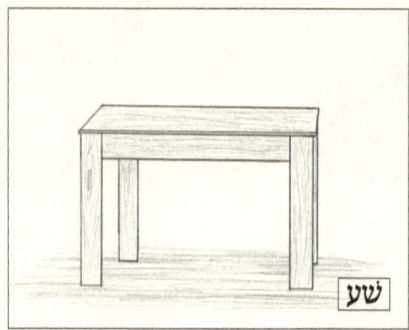

שֻׁלְחָן \ שֻׁלְחָנוֹת

וְשַׂמְתָּ אֶת־הַשֻּׁלְחָן מִחוּץ לַפָּרֹכֶת

סֵפֶר \ סְפָרִים

זֶה סֵפֶר תּוֹלְדֹת אָדָם

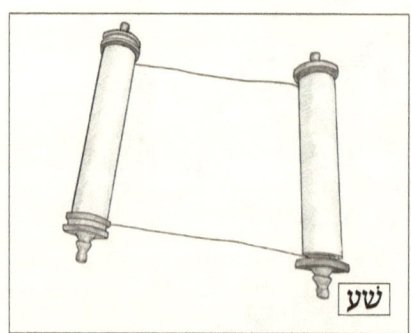

מְגִלָּה \ מְגִלּוֹת

אַחֲרֵי שְׂרֹף הַמֶּלֶךְ אֶת־הַמְּגִלָּה

---

shulxán / shulxanót
N: table (m)
"And you shall place the table outside the curtain." (Exod 26:35)

kisé / kis'ót
N: chair, throne (m)
"And let us set for him there a table and a chair." (2 Kgs 4:10)

məgilá / məgilót
N: scroll (f)
... after the king burned the scroll. (Jer 36:27)

séfer / sfarím
N: document, writing (m)
This is the document of the generations of Adam. (Gen 5:1)

Education 101

דִּבֶּר \ יְדַבֵּר   שָׁמַע \ יִשְׁמַע

פַּרְעֹה מְדַבֵּר אֶל־מֹשֶׁה וְאַהֲרֹן   גִּדְעוֹן שָׁמַע אֶת־מִסְפַּר הַחֲלוֹם

דבר | וַיְדַבֵּר | דַּבֵּר | דִּבֶּר   שמע | וַיִּשְׁמַע | שְׁמַע | שָׁמֹעַ

כָּתַב \ יִכְתֹּב   קָרָא \ יִקְרָא

בָּרוּךְ כָּתַב אֶת־דִּבְרֵי יְהוָה   אֵשֶׁת־פּוֹטִיפַר קֹרֵאת לָאֲנָשִׁים

כתב | וַיִּכְתֹּב | כְּתֹב | כָּתֹב   קרא | וַיִּקְרָא | קְרָא | קְרֹא

---

shamá / yishmá
Q: hear; obey
Gideon is hearing the telling of the dream. (Judg 7:15)

qará / yiqrá
Q: call out; read (aloud)
The wife of Potiphar is calling out to the men. (Gen 39:14)

dibér / yədabér
PI: speak
Pharaoh is speaking to Moses and Aaron. (Exod 7:9)

katáv / yixtóv
Q: write
Baruch is writing the words of YHWH. (Jer 36:4)

4
The Constructed Order

4.1
Building and Travel

עִיר \ עָרִים

לֵךְ אֶל־נִינְוֵה הָעִיר הַגְּדוֹלָה

בַּיִת \ בָּתִּים

אֵינֶנּוּ גָדוֹל בַּבַּיִת הַזֶּה מִמֶּנִּי

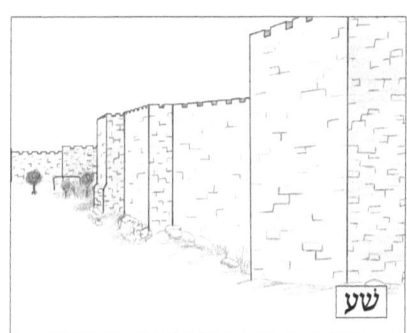

חוֹמָה \ חוֹמוֹת

וּבַחוֹמָה הִיא יוֹשָׁבֶת

שַׁעַר \ שְׁעָרִים

וְיִרַשׁ זַרְעֲךָ אֵת שַׁעַר אֹיְבָיו

ír / arím
N: city, town (f)
"Walk to Nineveh, the great city."
(Jon 1:2)

báyt / batím
N: house (m)
"There is no one greater in this
house than me." (Gen 39:9)

xomá / xomót
N: wall (of a city, typically) (f)
And in the city wall she was
dwelling. (Josh 2:15)

shá'ar / shə'arím
N: gate (m)
"And your seed shall possess the
gate of his enemies." (Gen 22:17)

חֶ֫דֶר \ חֲדָרִים

וַיָּבֹא הַחַ֫דְרָה וַיֵּבְךְּ שָׁ֫מָּה

קִיר \ קִירוֹת

וְהִנֵּה הַנֶּ֫גַע בְּקִירֹת הַבַּ֫יִת

דֶּ֫לֶת \ דְּלָתוֹת

וַיֵּצֵא לוֹט וְהַדֶּ֫לֶת סָגַר אַחֲרָיו

חַלּוֹן \ חַלּוֹנוֹת

וַתֹּ֫רֶד מִיכַל אֶת־דָּוִד בְּעַד הַחַלּוֹן

---

xéder / xadarím
N: room, chamber (m)
He entered into the room and wept there. (Gen 43:30)

qír / qirót
N: wall (of a house, typically) (m)
And behold the affliction was in the walls of the house. (Lev 14:37)

délet / dəlatót
N: door (f)
Lot went out, and he shut the door behind him. (Gen 19:6)

xalón / xalonót
N: window (f)
And Michal lowered David through the window. (1 Sam 19:12)

Building and Travel

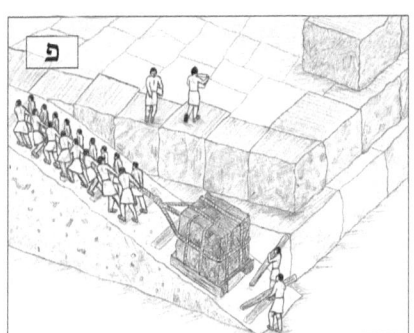

בָּנָה \ יִבְנֶה

בְּנֵי הָאָדָם בֹּנִים מִגְדָּל

בנה | וַיִּבֶן | בְּנֵה | בָּנוֹת

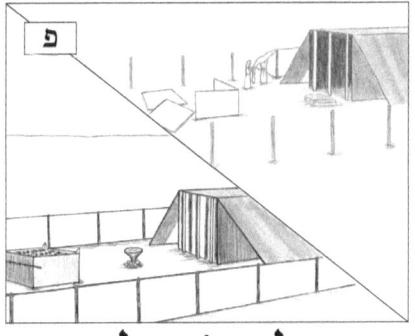

כָּלָה \ יִכְלֶה

*כָּל־עֲבֹדַת הַמִּשְׁכָּן כָּלְתָה

כלה | וַיְכַל | — | כְּלוֹת

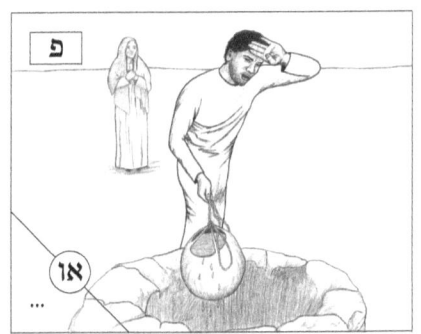

עָבַד \ יַעֲבֹד

יַעֲקֹב עָבַד בְּרָחֵל שֶׁבַע שָׁנִים

עבד | וַיַּעֲבֹד | עֲבֹד | עֲבֹד

נָח \ יָנוּחַ

הַתֵּבָה נָחָה עַל הָרֵי אֲרָרָט

נוח | וַיָּנַח | נוּחַ | נוֹחַ

baná / yivné
Q: build
The children of man are building a tower. (Gen 11:4)

kalá / yixlé
Q: be finished
All the work of the tabernacle was finished. (Exod 39:32)

avád / ya'avód
Q: work, serve
Jacob is working seven years for Rachel. (Gen 29:20)

náx / yanúax
Q: rest
The ark is resting on the mountains of Ararat. (Gen 8:4)

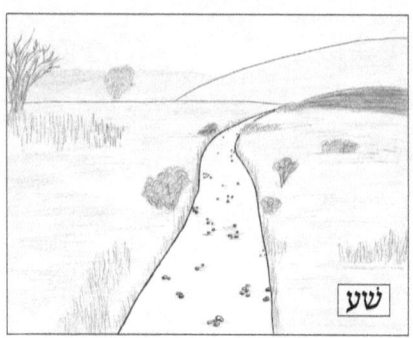 

דֶּרֶךְ \ דְּרָכִים   עֲגָלָה \ עֲגָלוֹת

וַיַּרְא אֶת־מַלְאַךְ יְהוָה נִצָּב בַּדֶּרֶךְ   וַיָּשִׂמוּ אֶת־הָאָרוֹן אֶל־הָעֲגָלָה

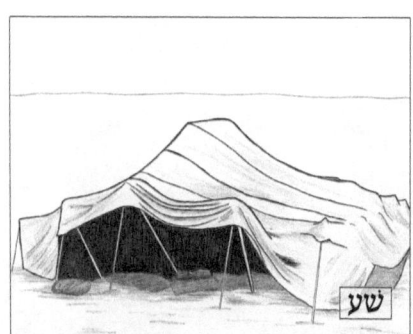 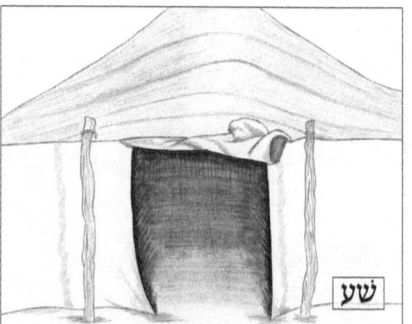

אֹהֶל \ אֹהָלִים   פֶּתַח \ פְּתָחִים

וַיָּבֹא לָבָן בְּאֹהֶל יַעֲקֹב   וְהוּא יֹשֵׁב פֶּתַח־הָאֹהֶל

dérex / draxím	agalá / agalót
N: path, way (f)	N: wagon, cart (f)
And he saw the angel of YHWH standing in the path. (Num 22:31)	And they placed the ark on the cart. (1 Sam 6:11)
óhel / ohalím	pétax / pətaxím
N: tent (m)	N: opening (m)
And Laban entered into the tent of Jacob. (Gen 31:33)	And he was sitting at the opening of the tent. (Gen 18:1)

Building and Travel

הִתְהַלֵּךְ \ יִתְהַלֵּךְ

אַבְרָם מִתְהַלֵּךְ בְּאֶרֶץ־כְּנָעַן

הלך | וַיִּתְהַלֵּךְ | הִתְהַלֵּךְ | הִתְהַלֵּךְ

נָסַע \ יִסַּע

אַבְרָהָם נָסַע אַרְצָה הַנֶּגֶב

נסע | וַיִּסַּע | סַע | נְסֹעַ

שָׁכַן \ יִשְׁכֹּן

אַבְרָם שָׁכַן בְּאֵלֹנֵי מַמְרֵא

שכן | וַיִּשְׁכֹּן | שְׁכֹן | שָׁכַן

חָנָה \ יַחֲנֶה

בְּנֵי יִשְׂרָאֵל חֹנִים עַל־הַיָּם

חנה | וַיִּחַן | חֲנֵה | חֲנוֹת

---

nasá / yisá
Q: journey, depart
Abraham is journeying to the land
of the Negev. (Gen 20:1)

hithaléx / yithaléx
HTP: walk about
Abram is walking about in the land
of Canaan. (Gen 13:17)

xaná / yaxané
Q: set up camp, encamp
The children of Israel are encamping
by the sea. (Exod 14:9)

shaxán / yishkón
Q: dwell
Abram is dwelling among the oaks
of Mamre. (Gen 14:13)

4.2 Measurement and Numbers

Measurement and Numbers 111

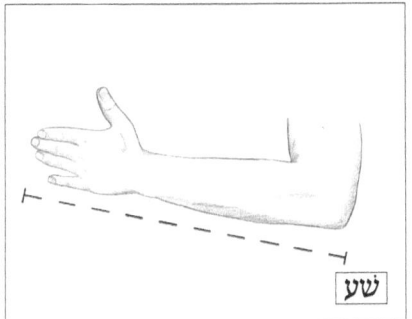

שְׁקֶל \ שְׁקָלִים

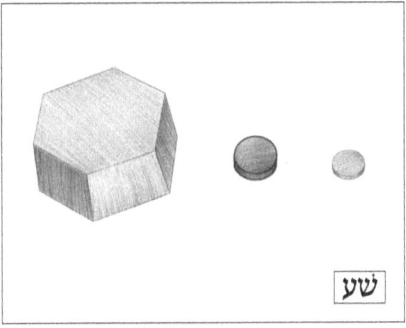

אַמָּה \ אַמּוֹת

וְעָשִׂיתָ שֻׁלְחָן אַמָּה רָחְבּוֹ

שְׂעַר רֹאשׁוֹ מָאתַיִם שְׁקָלִים

אֵיפָה

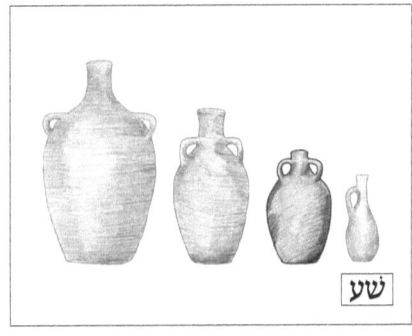

הִין

וַיֹּאמֶר יִשַׁי לְדָוִד קַח אֵיפַת הַקָּלִיא

וְיַיִן תַּקְרִיב חֲצִי הַהִין

---

amá / amót
N: cubit (~18 inches) (f)
"And you shall make a table, a cubit its width." (Exod 25:23)

shéqel / shqalím
N: shekel (~.4 ounces) (m)
The hair of his head was 200 shekels. (2 Sam 14:26)

efá
N: ephah (~20 dry quarts) (f)
And Jesse said to David, "Take the ephah of roasted grain." (1 Sam 17:17)

hín
N: hin (~1 gallon) (f)
"And you shall bring near wine, half of the hin." (Num 15:10)

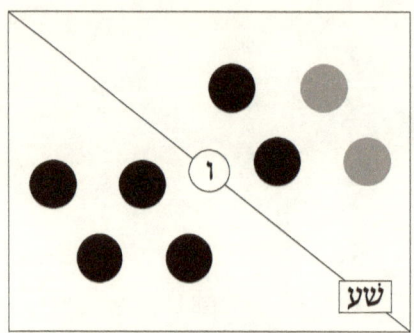 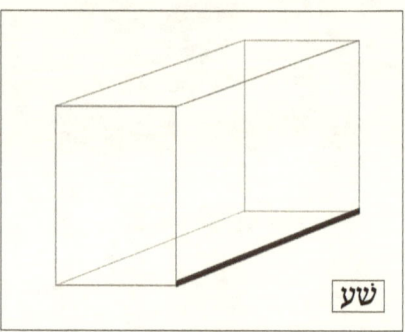

חֲצִי · כֹּל　　　　　אֹרֶךְ

בַּחֲצִי הַלַּיְלָה וַיַּךְ כָּל־בְּכוֹר　　וְעָשִׂיתָ שֻׁלְחָן אַמָּתַיִם אָרְכּוֹ

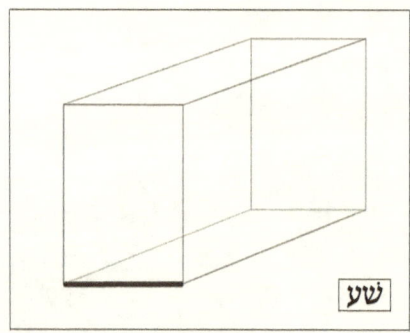 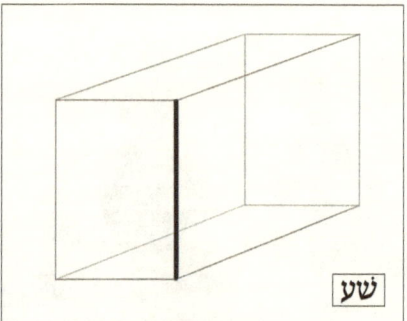

רֹחַב　　　　　קוֹמָה

וְאַמָּה רָחְבּוֹ　　וְאַמָּה וָחֵצִי קֹמָתוֹ

---

xatsí / kól
N: half, middle; all, each, every
In the middle of the night, he struck every firstborn. (Exod 12:29)

órex
N: length
"And you shall make a table, two cubits its length ..." (Exod 25:23)

róxav
N: width
"... and a cubit its width ..."
(Exod 25:23)

qomá
N: height
"... and a cubit and a half its height."
(Exod 25:23)

 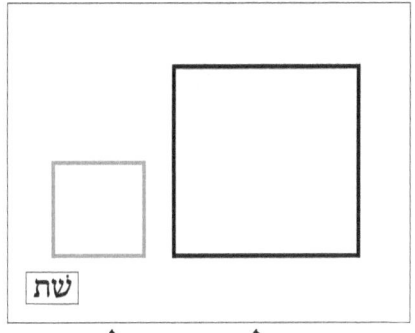

כָּבֵד \ כְּבֵדָה   גָּדוֹל \ גְּדוֹלָה

כִּי־כָבֵד מִמְּךָ הַדָּבָר   וְאַבְרָהָם הָיוֹ יִהְיֶה לְגוֹי גָּדוֹל

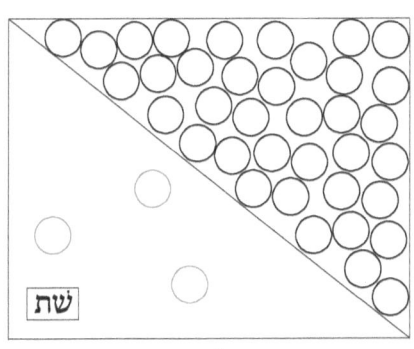 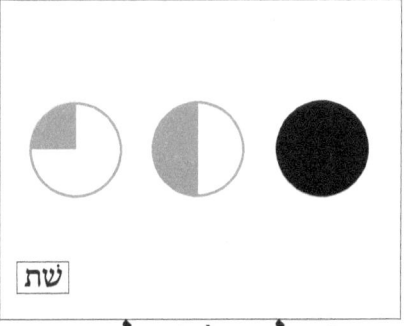

רַב \ רַבָּה   שָׁלֵם \ שְׁלֵמָה

וַנֵּשֶׁב בְּמִצְרַיִם יָמִים רַבִּים   הִתְהַלַּכְתִּי לְפָנֶיךָ בְּלֵבָב שָׁלֵם

---

kavéd / kəvedá
ADJ: heavy; honored (m/f)
"... because the thing is too heavy for you." (Exod 18:18)

gadól / gədolá
ADJ: big, great (m/f)
"And Abraham shall surely become a great nation." (Gen 18:18)

ráv / rabá
ADJ: much, many; great (m/f)
"And we dwelt in Egypt many days." (Num 20:15)

shalém / shlemá
ADJ: whole, complete (m/f)
"I have walked about before you with a whole heart." (2 Kgs 20:3)

רִאשׁוֹן \ רִאשֹׁנָה

זֶה יָצָא רִאשֹׁנָה

שֵׁנִי \ שֵׁנִית

וַיָּסֹבּוּ אֶת־הָעִיר בַּיּוֹם הַשֵּׁנִי

שְׁלִישִׁי \ שְׁלִישִׁית

וַיְצַו אֶת־הַשֵּׁנִי וְאֶת־הַשְּׁלִישִׁי

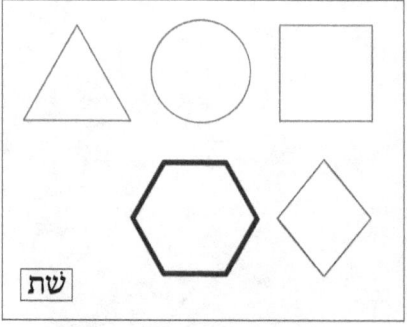

אַחֵר \ אַחֶרֶת

וְהִנֵּה שֶׁבַע פָּרוֹת אֲחֵרוֹת עֹלוֹת

---

rishón / rishoná
ADJ: first (m/f)
"This one came out first."
(Gen 38:28)

shení / shenít
ADJ: second (m/f)
And they went around the city on
the second day. (Josh 6:14)

shlishí / shlishít
ADJ: third (m/f)
He commanded the second (man)
and the third (man). (Gen 32:20*)

axér / axéret
ADJ: other, another (m/f)
And, behold, seven other cows were
coming up. (Gen 41:3)

Measurement and Numbers

סָפַר \ יִסְפֹּר

אַבְרָם סָפַר אֶת־הַכּוֹכָבִים

ספר | וַיִּסְפֹּר | סָפֹר | סְפֹר

יָסַף \ יֹסֵף

מֹשֶׁה יֹסֵף עוֹד שָׁלֹשׁ עָרִים

יסף | — | סֹף | —

קָנָה \ יִקְנֶה

פּוֹטִיפַר קָנָה אֶת־יוֹסֵף

קנה | וַיִּקֶן | קָנֹה | קְנוֹת

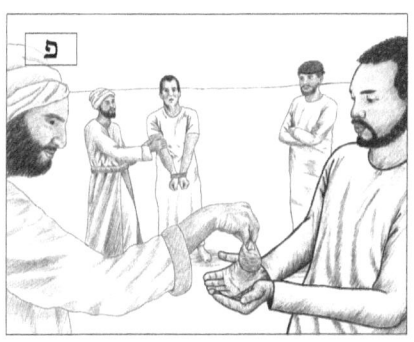

מָכַר \ יִמְכֹּר

אֲחֵי יוֹסֵף מֹכְרִים אֹתוֹ

מכר | וַיִּמְכֹּר | מָכֹר | מְכֹר

---

safár / yispór
Q: count
Abram is counting the stars.
(Gen 15:5)

yasáf
Q: add, do again
Moses is adding another three cities.
(Deut 19:9)

qaná / yiqné
Q: buy, acquire
Potiphar is buying Joseph.
(Gen 39:1)

maxár / yimkór
Q: sell
Joseph's brothers are selling him.
(Gen 37:28)

9 276 14 [שע]	1 [שת]
מִסְפָּר אֲבָנִים כְּמִסְפַּר שִׁבְטֵי יִשְׂרָאֵל	אֶחָד \ אַחַת וַיְהִי כָל־הָאָרֶץ שָׂפָה אֶחָת
2 [שע]	3 [שע]
שְׁנַיִם \ שְׁתַּיִם שְׁנַיִם מִכֹּל תָּבִיא אֶל־הַתֵּבָה	שְׁלֹשָׁה \ שָׁלוֹשׁ וַיַּרְא וְהִנֵּה שְׁלֹשָׁה אֲנָשִׁים

mispár
N: number (m)
... stones according to the number of the tribes of Israel. (1 Kgs 18:31)

exád / axát
ADJ: one (m/f)
All of the earth was one language. (Gen 11:1)

shnáym / shtáym
N: two (m/f)
"Two of everything you shall bring to the ark." (Gen 6:19)

shloshá / shalósh
N: three (m/f)
He looked, and behold, there were three men. (Gen 18:2)

4

אַרְבָּעָה \ אַרְבַּע

וְעָשִׂיתָ קַרְנֹתָיו עַל אַרְבַּע פִּנֹּתָיו

5

חֲמִשָּׁה \ חָמֵשׁ

וַיָּנֻסוּ חֲמֵשֶׁת הַמְּלָכִים הָאֵלֶּה

6

שִׁשָּׁה \ שֵׁשׁ

יָלַדְתִּי לוֹ שִׁשָּׁה בָנִים

7

שִׁבְעָה \ שֶׁבַע

שֶׁבַע פָּרֹת שֶׁבַע שָׁנִים הֵנָּה

arba'á / arbá
N: four (m/f)
"And you shall make its horns on its four corners." (Exod 27:2)

xamishá / xamésh
N: five (m/f)
And these five kings fled.
(Josh 10:16)

shishá / shésh
N: six (m/f)
"I have borne for him six sons."
(Gen 30:20)

shiv'á / shéva
N: seven (m/f)
"Seven cows are seven years."
(Gen 41:26)

8

שע

שְׁמֹנָה \ שְׁמֹנֶה

וַיָּמָל אֶת־יִצְחָק בֶּן־שְׁמֹנַת יָמִים

9

שע

תִּשְׁעָה \ תֵּשַׁע

לְתִשְׁעַת הַמַּטּוֹת וַחֲצִי הַמַּטֶּה

10

שע

עֲשָׂרָה \ עֶשֶׂר

אוּלַי יִמָּצְאוּן שָׁם עֲשָׂרָה

11 12 13 14 15 16 17 18 19

שע

־עָשָׂר \ ־עֶשְׂרֵה

שְׁתֵּי עֶשְׂרֵה שָׁנָה שְׁנֵי־עָשָׂר חֹדֶשׁ

---

shmoná / shmoné
N: eight (m/f)
And he circumcised Isaac at eight days old. (Gen 21:4)

tish'á / tésha
N: nine (m/f)
... to the nine tribes and half of the tribe. (Num 34:13)

asará / éser
N: ten (m/f)
"Perhaps ten are found there." (Gen 18:32)

asár / esré
N: -teen (m/f)
... the twelfth year, the twelfth month. (Ezek 32:1)

20

עֶשְׂרִים

שָׁפַט אֶת־יִשְׂרָאֵל עֶשְׂרִים שָׁנָה

50

חֲמִשִּׁים

אוּלַי יֵשׁ חֲמִשִּׁים צַדִּיקִם בָּעִיר

100

מֵאָה \ מֵאוֹת

וְאַבְרָהָם בֶּן־מְאַת שָׁנָה

1000

אֶלֶף \ אֲלָפִים

הִנֵּה נָתַתִּי אֶלֶף כֶּסֶף לְאָחִיךְ

---

esrím
N: twenty
He judged Israel for twenty years. (Judg 16:31)

xamishím
N: fifty
"Perhaps there are fifty righteous in the city." (Gen 18:24)

me'á / me'ót
N: hundred (f)
And Abraham was one hundred years old. (Gen 21:5)

élef / alafím
N: thousand (m)
"Behold, I give a thousand (pieces of) silver to your brother." (Gen 20:16)

5
Word Groups

5.1
Movement Verbs

יָצָא \ יֵצֵא

בַּת־יִפְתָּח יֹצֵאת לִקְרָאתוֹ

יצא | וַיֵּצֵא | צֵא | צֵאת

בָּא \ יָבוֹא

שְׁנַיִם שְׁנַיִם הֵם בָּאִים אֶל־נֹחַ

בוא | וַיָּבֹא | בֹּא | בֹּא

סָר \ יָסוּר

מֹשֶׁה סָר לִרְאוֹת אֶת־הַסְּנֶה

סור | וַיָּסַר | סוּר | סוּר

שָׁב \ יָשׁוּב

הַיּוֹנָה שָׁבָה אֶל־הַתֵּבָה

שוב | וַיָּשָׁב | שׁוּב | שׁוּב

---

yatsá / yetsé
Q: go out
Jepthah's daughter is going out to meet him. (Judg 11:34)

bá / yavó
Q: come, enter
Two by two they are coming to Noah. (Gen 7:9)

sár / yasúr
Q: turn aside
Moses is turning aside to see the bush. (Exod 3:3)

sháv / yashúv
Q: return
The dove is returning to the ark. (Gen 8:9)

Word Groups

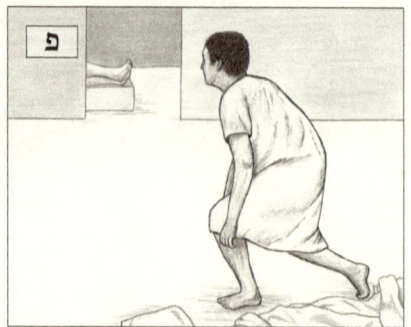

קָם \ יָקוּם

שְׁמוּאֵל קָם לָלֶכֶת אֶל־עֵלִי

קוּם | וַיָּקָם | קוּם | קוּם

יָשַׁב \ יֵשֵׁב

יוֹנָה יָשַׁב תַּחַת הַסֻּכָּה

ישׁב | וַיֵּשֶׁב | שֵׁב | שָׁבַת

עָמַד \ יַעֲמֹד

מֹשֶׁה עָמַד עַל־אַדְמַת קֹדֶשׁ

עמד | וַיַּעֲמֹד | עֲמֹד | עָמַד

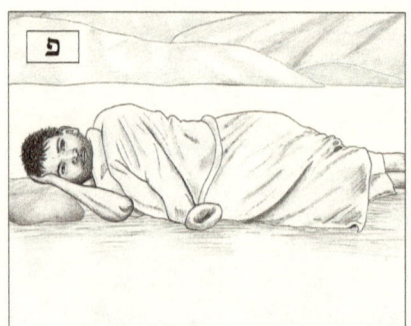

שָׁכַב \ יִשְׁכַּב

יַעֲקֹב שָׁכַב עַל־אֶבֶן

שׁכב | וַיִּשְׁכַּב | שְׁכַב | שָׁכַב

---

yasháv / yeshév
Q: sit; dwell
Jonah is sitting under the shelter.
(Jon 4:5)

qám / yaqúm
Q: arise, get up
Samuel is getting up to walk to Eli.
(1 Sam 3:6)

shaxáv / yishkáv
Q: lie down
Jacob is lying down on a rock.
(Gen 28:11)

amád / ya'amód
Q: stand
Moses is standing on holy ground.
(Exod 3:5)

עָלָה \ יַעֲלֶה

מֹשֶׁה עָלָה אֶל־רֹאשׁ הָהָר

עלה | וַיַּעַל | עָלָה | עֲלוֹת

יָרַד \ יֵרֵד

יוֹנָה יָרַד אֶל־יַרְכְּתֵי הַסְּפִינָה

ירד | וַיֵּרֶד | רֵד | רֶדֶת

הָלַךְ \ יֵלֵךְ

אַבְרָהָם וְיִצְחָק הֹלְכִים אֶל־הָהָר

הלך | וַיֵּלֶךְ | לֵךְ | לֶכֶת

רָץ \ יָרוּץ

אֲחִימַעַץ רָץ אֶל־דָּוִד

רוץ | וַיָּרָץ | רוּץ | רוּץ

---

alá / ya'alé
Q: go up
Moses is going up to the top of the mountain. (Exod 19:20)

yarád / yeréd
Q: go down
Jonah is going down into the rear parts of the ship. (Jon 1:5)

haláx / yeléx
Q: walk, go
Abraham and Isaac are walking to the mountain. (Gen 22:8)

ráts / yarúts
Q: run
Ahimaaz is running to David. (2 Sam 18:19)

Word Groups

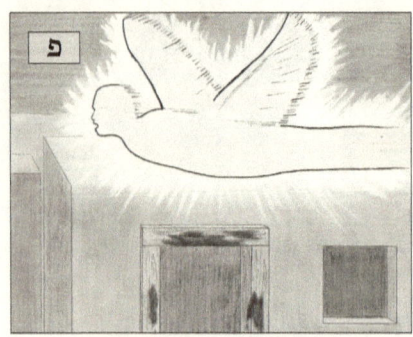

עָבַר \ יַעֲבֹר

מַלְאַךְ יְהוָה עֹבֵר בְּאֶרֶץ־מִצְרַיִם

עבר | וַיַּעֲבֹר | עָבַר | עֹבֵר

סָבַב \ יָסֹב

כָּל הָאֲנָשִׁים סֹבְבִים אֶת־הָעִיר

סבב | וַיִּסֹּב | סֹב | סָבַב

פָּנָה \ יִפְנֶה

פַּרְעֹה פָּנָה מֵעִם מֹשֶׁה וְאַהֲרֹן

פנה | וַיִּפֶן | פְּנֵה | פְּנוֹת

קָרַב \ יִקְרַב

אֶסְתֵּר קְרֵבָת אֶל־הַמֶּלֶךְ

קרב | וַיִּקְרַב | קָרַב | קָרֹב

---

avár / ya'avór
Q: pass over, pass by
The angel of YHWH is passing over the land of Egypt. (Exod 12:12)

savάv / yasόv
Q: go around
All of the men are going around the city. (Josh 6:3)

paná / yifné
Q: turn
Pharaoh is turning away from Moses and Aaron. (Exod 7:23)

qaráv / yiqráv
Q: come near
Esther is coming near to the king. (Esth 5:2)

Movement Verbs

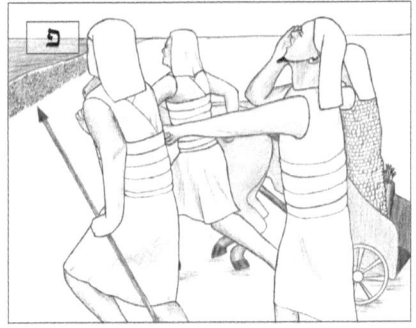

רָדַף \ יִרְדֹּף

מִצְרַיִם רֹדְפִים אַחֲרֵי בְּנֵי יִשְׂרָאֵל

רדף | וַיִּרְדֹּף | רָדַף | רְדֹף

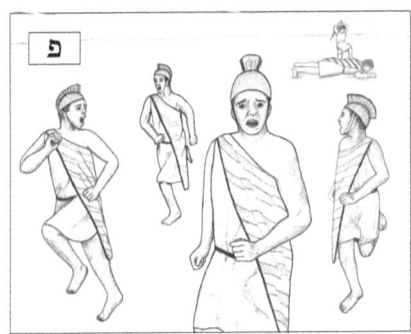

נָס \ יָנוּס

הַפְּלִשְׁתִּים נָסִים מִפְּנֵי דָוִד

נוס | וַיָּנָס | נוּס | נוּס

נִשְׁאַר \ יִשָּׁאֵר

נָעֳמִי נִשְׁאֶרֶת מִיְּלָדֶיהָ וּמֵאִישָׁהּ

שאר | וַיִּשָּׁאֵר | — | —

גָּלָה \ יִגְלֶה

יִשְׂרָאֵל גָּלָה מֵעַל אַדְמָתוֹ אַשּׁוּרָה

גלה | וַיִּגֶל | גָּלֹה | גָּלוֹת

radáf / yirdóf
Q: pursue, chase
Egypt is chasing after the children of Israel. (Exod 14:9)

nish'ár / yisha'ér
NI: remain, be left over
Naomi is left without her boys and without her husband. (Ruth 1:5)

nás / yanús
Q: flee
The Philistines are fleeing before David. (1 Sam 17:51)

galá / yiglé
Q: depart (into exile)
Israel is going into exile from its ground to Assyria. (2 Kgs 17:23)

5.2
Action and Stative Verbs

Action and Stative Verbs

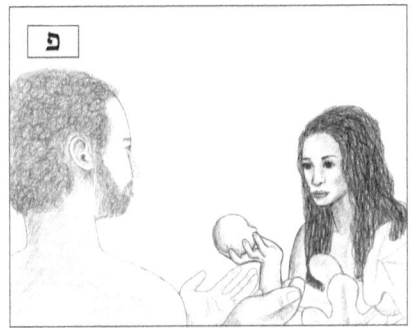

נָתַן \ יִתֵּן

חַוָּה נֹתֶנֶת אֶת־הַפְּרִי לְאִישָׁהּ

נתן | וַיִּתֵּן | תֵּן | תֵּת

לָקַח \ יִקַּח

שִׁמְשׁוֹן לֹקֵחַ לְחִי־חֲמוֹר

לקח | וַיִּקַּח | קַח | קַחַת

שָׂם \ יָשִׂים

אַבְרָהָם שָׂם אֹתוֹ עַל־הַמִּזְבֵּחַ

שים | וַיָּשֶׂם | שִׂים | שִׂים

נָשָׂא \ יִשָּׂא

בְּנֵי־יִשְׂרָאֵל נֹשְׂאִים אֲבָנִים

נשא | וַיִּשָּׂא | שָׂא | שְׂאֵת\נְשׂא

---

laqáx / yiqáx
Q: take, grab
Samson is taking a jawbone of a donkey. (Judg 15:15)

natán / yitén
Q: give
Eve is giving the fruit to her husband. (Gen 3:6)

nasá / yisá
Q: pick up; carry
The children of Israel are picking up stones. (Josh 4:8)

sám / yasím
Q: set down, place
Abraham is placing him on the altar. (Gen 22:9)

Word Groups

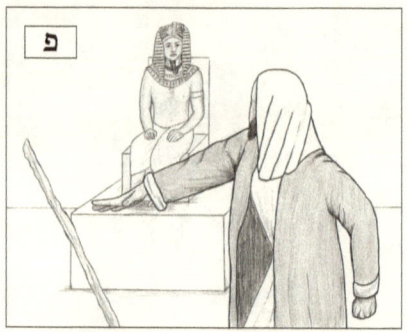

הִשְׁלִיךְ \ יַשְׁלִיךְ

אַהֲרֹן מַשְׁלִיךְ מַטֵּהוּ לִפְנֵי פַרְעֹה

שׁלך | וַיַּשְׁלֵךְ | הַשְׁלֵךְ | הַשְׁלִיךְ

לָכַד \ יִלְכֹּד

שִׁמְשׁוֹן לֹכֵד שׁוּעָל

לכד | וַיִּלְכֹּד | לְכֹד | לָכֹד

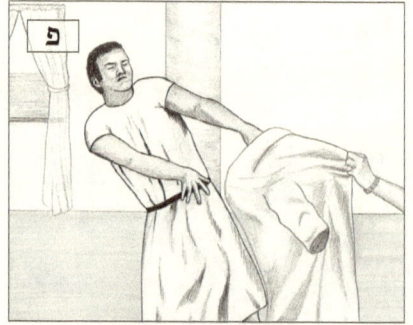

עָזַב \ יַעֲזֹב

יוֹסֵף עָזַב בִּגְדוֹ בְּיַד־אֵשֶׁת אֲדֹנָיו

עזב | וַיַּעֲזֹב | עֲזֹב | עָזֹב

בָּחַר \ יִבְחַר

דָּוִד בָּחַר לוֹ חָמֵשׁ אֲבָנִים

בחר | וַיִּבְחַר | בְּחַר | בָּחֹר

---

laxád / yilkód
Q: seize, catch
Samson is seizing a fox.
(Judg 15:4)

hishlíx / yashlíx
HI: throw
Aaron is throwing his staff before
Pharaoh. (Exod 7:10)

baxár / yivxár
Q: choose
David is choosing for himself five
stones. (1 Sam 17:40)

azáv / ya'azóv
Q: leave, forsake
Joseph is leaving his garment in the
hand of his master's wife. (Gen 39:12)

Action and Stative Verbs 131

סָגַר \ יִסְגֹּר

הַמַּלְאָכִים סֹגְרִים אֶת־דֶּלֶת הַבַּיִת

סגר | וַיִּסְגֹּר | סָגַר | סָגַר

פָּתַח \ יִפְתַּח

נֹחַ פָּתַח אֶת־חַלּוֹן הַתֵּבָה

פתח | וַיִּפְתַּח | פָּתַח | פְּתַח

שָׁפַךְ \ יִשְׁפֹּךְ

מֹשֶׁה שָׁפַךְ מַיִם עַל־הַיַּבָּשָׁה

שפך | וַיִּשְׁפֹּךְ | שָׁפַךְ | שְׁפֹךְ

אָסַף \ יֶאֱסֹף

הָעָם אֹסְפִים אֶת־הַשְּׂלָו

אסף | וַיֶּאֱסֹף | אֱסֹף | אֱסֹף

---

sagár / yisgór
Q: close
The angels are shutting the door of the house. (Gen 19:10)

patáx / yiftáx
Q: open
Noah is opening the window of the ark. (Gen 8:6)

shafáx / yishpóx
Q: pour out
Moses is pouring water onto the dry ground. (Exod 4:9)

asáf / ye'esóf
Q: gather
The people are gathering the quail. (Num 11:32)

Word Groups

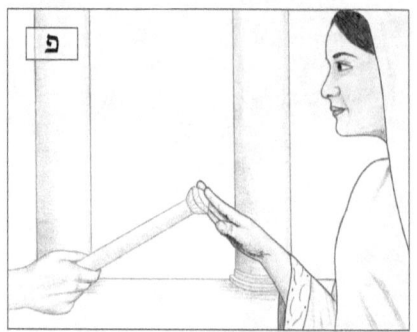

רָאָה \ יִרְאֶה   נָגַע \ יִגַּע

חַוָּה רֹאָה כִּי טוֹב הָעֵץ לְמַאֲכָל   אֶסְתֵּר נֹגַעַת בְּרֹאשׁ הַשַּׁרְבִיט

ראה | וַיַּרְא | רָאָה | רְאוֹת   נגע | וַיִּגַּע | גַּע | נֹגַעַ\גַּעַת

הֵחֵל \ יָחֵל   כִּלָּה \ יְכַלֶּה

מִצְרִי מֵחֵל בַּגָּדוֹל   בְּנֵי יַעֲקֹב מְכַלִּים אֶת־הַשֶּׁבֶר

חלל | וַיָּחֶל | הָחֵל | הָחֵל   כלה | וַיְכַל | כַּלֵּה | כַּלּוֹת

---

raʾá / yirʾé
Q: see
Eve sees that the tree is good for food. (Gen 3:6)

nagá / yigá
Q: touch
Esther is touching the head of the scepter. (Esth 5:2)

hexél / yaxél
HI: begin
An Egyptian is beginning with the oldest. (Gen 44:12)

kilá / yəxalé
PI: complete, finish
The sons of Jacob are finishing the grain. (Gen 43:2)

Action and Stative Verbs

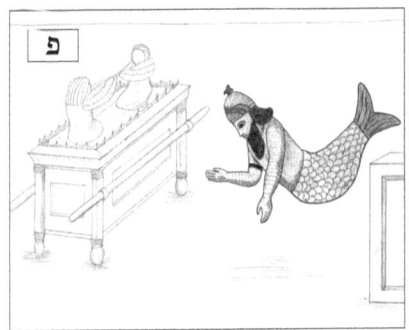

נָפַל \ יִפֹּל

דָּגוֹן נֹפֵל לִפְנֵי אֲרוֹן יְהוָה

נפל | וַיִּפֹּל | נָפַל | נֹפֵל

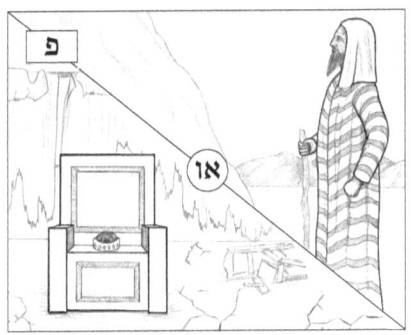

נָכוֹן \ יִכּוֹן

מֹשֶׁה נָכוֹן לַעֲלֹת אֶל־הַר סִינַי

כון | וַיִּכּוֹן | הִכּוֹן | —

מָלֵא \ יִמְלָא

הַכְּלִי מָלֵא שֶׁמֶן

מלא | וַיִּמְלָא | מָלֵא | מְלֵאת

חָסֵר \ יֶחְסַר

*צַפַּחַת הַשֶּׁמֶן חָסֵרָה

חסר | וַיֶּחְסַר | — | —

nafál / yipól
Q: fall
Dagon is falling before the ark of YHWH. (1 Sam 5:3)

malé / yimlá
Q: be full
The vessel is full of oil.
(2 Kgs 4:6)

naxón / yikón
NI: be ready; be established
Moses is ready to go up to Mount Sinai. (Exod 34:2)

xasér / yexsár
Q: be lacking, be empty
The jug of oil was empty.
(1 Kgs 17:14)

Word Groups

שָׂנֵא \ יִשְׂנָא

אֲחֵי יוֹסֵף שֹׂנְאִים אֹתוֹ

שׂנא | וַיִּשְׂנָא | שָׂנֵא | שְׂנֹא

אָהַב \ יֶאֱהַב

יַעֲקֹב אָהַב אֶת־רָחֵל מִלֵּאָה

אהב | וַיֶּאֱהַב | אָהַב | אַהֲבָה\אָהֵב

בָּכָה \ יִבְכֶּה

עֵשָׂו בֹּכֶה כִּי אֵין לְאָבִיו בְּרָכָה

בכה | וַיֵּבְךְּ | בָּכָה | בְּכוֹת

שָׂמַח \ יִשְׂמַח

יוֹנָה שָׂמֵחַ עַל־הַקִּיקָיוֹן

שׂמח | וַיִּשְׂמַח | שָׂמַח | שְׂמֹחַ

---

aháv / ye'eháv
Q: love
Jacob loves Rachel more than Leah.
(Gen 29:30)

sané / yisná
Q: hate
Joseph's brothers hate him.
(Gen 37:4)

samáx / yismáx
Q: be glad, be happy
Jonah is happy concerning the plant.
(Jon 4:6)

baxá / yivké
Q: cry, weep
Esau is crying because his father
does not have a blessing. (Gen 27:38)

Action and Stative Verbs

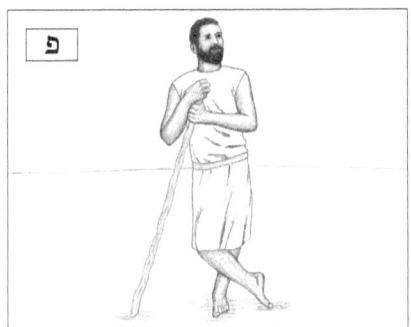

בָּטַח \ יִבְטַח

אִישׁ בֹּטֵחַ עַל־מִשְׁעֶנֶת

בטח | וַיִּבְטַח | בָּטַח | בֹּטֵחַ

יָרֵא \ יִירָא

אַנְשֵׁי יִשְׂרָאֵל יְרֵאִים מִפְּנֵי גָלְיָת

ירא | וַיִּירָא | יָרֵא | יְרֵאָה

be able

יָכֹל \ יוּכַל

*לֹא־יוּכַל הַנַּעַר לַעֲזֹב אֶת־אָבִיו

יכל | וַיֻּכַל | — | יְכֹלֶת

בּוֹשׁ \ יֵבוֹשׁ

הַבֹּטֵחַ בַּפֶּסֶל בּוֹשׁ

בוש | וַיֵּבוֹשׁ | בּוֹשׁ | בּוֹשׁ

---

batáx / yivtáx
Q: trust, rely
A man is trusting in a staff.
(2 Kgs 18:21)

yaxól / yuxál
Q: be able
The young man is not able to leave his father. (Gen 44:22)

yaré / yirá
Q: fear
The people of Israel are fearing before Goliath. (1 Sam 17:24)

bósh / yevósh
Q: be ashamed
The one who trusts in the idol is ashamed. (Isa 42:17)

5.3
Derived Binyanim

Derived Binyanim

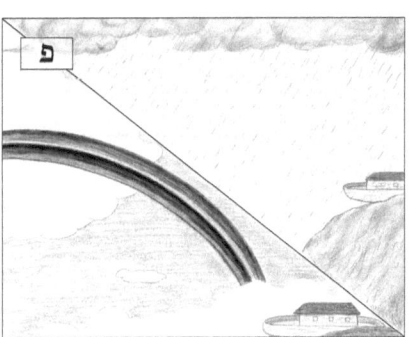

נִרְאָה \ יֵרָאֶה

הַקֶּשֶׁת נִרְאָה בֶּעָנָן

ראה | וַיֵּרָא | הֵרָאֶה | הֵרָאוֹת

נִמְצָא \ יִמָּצֵא

הַגָּבִיעַ נִמְצָא בְּאַמְתַּחַת בִּנְיָמִן

מצא | וַיִּמָּצֵא | — | הִמָּצֵא

הִתְחַזֵּק \ יִתְחַזֵּק

דָּוִד מִתְחַזֵּק בַּיהוָה אֱלֹהָיו

חזק | וַיִּתְחַזֵּק | הִתְחַזֵּק | הִתְחַזֵּק

הִתְהַלֵּל \ יִתְהַלֵּל

אִישׁ מִתְהַלֵּל בְּחָכְמָתוֹ וּבִגְבוּרָתוֹ

הלל | וַיִּתְהַלֵּל | הִתְהַלֵּל | הִתְהַלֵּל

---

nir'á / yera'é
NI: appear
The rainbow appears in the clouds.
(Gen 9:14)

nimtsá / yimatsé
NI: be found
The cup is found in the sack of Benjamin. (Gen 44:12)

hitxazéq / yitxazéq
HTP: strengthen oneself
David is strengthening himself in YHWH his God. (1 Sam 30:6)

hithalél / yithalél
HTP: boast (praise oneself)
A man is boasting in his wisdom and in his strength. (Jer 9:22*)

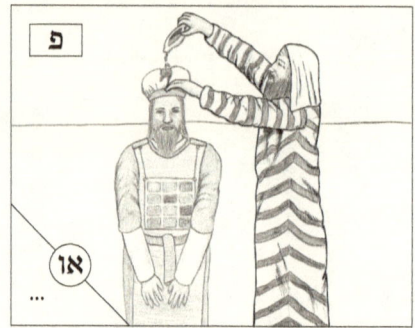

קַדֵּשׁ \ יְקַדֵּשׁ
מֹשֶׁה מְקַדֵּשׁ אֶת־אַהֲרֹן לַיהוָה
קדש | וַיְקַדֵּשׁ | קַדֵּשׁ | קַדֵּשׁ

חִזַּק \ יְחַזֵּק
יְהוָה מְחַזֵּק אֶת־שִׁמְשׁוֹן
חזק | וַיְחַזֵּק | חַזֵּק | חַזֵּק

שִׁלַּם \ יְשַׁלֵּם
הָאִשָּׁה מְשַׁלֶּמֶת אֶת־נִשְׁיָהּ
שלם | — | שַׁלֵּם | שַׁלֵּם

מִלֵּא \ יְמַלֵּא
מִצְרִי מְמַלֵּא אֶת־הָאַמְתַּחַת אֹכֶל
מלא | וַיְמַלֵּא | מַלֵּא | מַלֵּא

---

xizáq / yəxazéq
PI: strengthen
YHWH is strengthening Samson.
(Judg 16:28)

qidásh / yəqadésh
PI: consecrate, make holy
Moses is consecrating Aaron to
YHWH. (Exod 40:13)

milé / yəmalé
PI: fill
An Egyptian is filling the sacks with
food. (Gen 44:1)

shilám / yəshalém
PI: (re)pay, make whole
The woman is paying her debt.
(2 Kgs 4:7)

Derived Binyanim   139

נִחַם \ יְנַחֵם

כָּל־בְּנֵי יַעֲקֹב מְנַחֲמִים אֹתוֹ

נחם | וַיְנַחֵם | נִחַם | נַחֵם

כִּבֵּד \ יְכַבֵּד

אִישׁ מְכַבֵּד אֱלוֹהַּ בְּזָהָב וּבְכֶסֶף

כבד | וַיְכַבֵּד | כַּבֵּד | כַּבֵּד

שִׁלַּח \ יְשַׁלַּח

אִישׁ מְשַׁלֵּחַ אֶת־הַשָּׂעִיר בַּמִּדְבָּר

שלח | וַיְשַׁלַּח | שַׁלַּח | שַׁלַּח

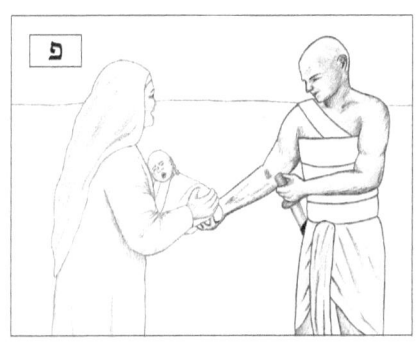

חִיָּה \ יְחַיֶּה

הַמִּצְרִי מְחַיֶּה אֶת־הַבַּת

חיה | וַיְחַיֶּה | חַיֵּה | חַיּוֹת

---

nixám / yənaxém
PI: comfort
All of Jacob's sons are comforting him. (Gen 37:35)

kibéd / yəxabéd
PI: honor
A man is honoring a god with gold and with silver. (Dan 11:38)

shiláx / yəshaláx
PI: send away
A man is sending away the goat in the wilderness. (Lev 16:22)

xiyá / yəxayé
PI: let live; give life
The Egyptian is letting the daughter live. (Exod 1:22)

Word Groups

הַקְרִיב \ יַקְרִיב

מֹשֶׁה מַקְרִיב אֶת אֵיל הָעֹלָה

קרב | וַיַּקְרֵב | הַקְרֵב | הַקְרִיב

הִכְרִית \ יַכְרִית

אִישׁ מַכְרִית אֶת־הַפָּסִיל

כרת | וַיַּכְרֵת | הַכְרֵת | הַכְרִית

הִשְׁמִיעַ \ יַשְׁמִיעַ

הַמֶּלֶךְ מַשְׁמִיעַ אֶת־כָּל־יְהוּדָה

שמע | וַיַּשְׁמַע | הַשְׁמַע | הַשְׁמִיעַ

הֶחֱזִיק \ יַחֲזִיק

אֲדֹנִיָּהוּ מַחֲזִיק בְּקַרְנוֹת הַמִּזְבֵּחַ

חזק | וַיַּחֲזֵק | הַחֲזֵק | הַחֲזִיק

hiqrív / yaqrív
HI: bring near
Moses is bringing near the ram of the burnt offering. (Lev 8:18)

hixrít / yaxrít
HI: cut off
A man is cutting down the idol. (Mic 5:12*)

hishmía / yashmía
HI: proclaim (cause to hear)
The king is proclaiming to all of Judah. (1 Kgs 15:22)

hexezíq / yaxazíq
HI: hold tightly; strengthen
Adonijah is holding tightly to the horns of the altar. (1 Kgs 1:50)

Derived Binyanim

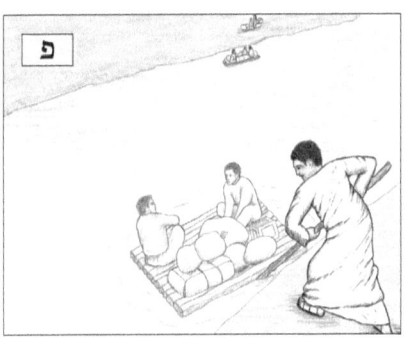

הֶעֱבִיר \ יַעֲבִיר

יַעֲקֹב מַעֲבִיר אֹתָם אֶת־הַנָּהָר

עבר | וַיַּעֲבֵר | הַעֲבֵר | הַעֲבִיר

הֶעֱמִיד \ יַעֲמִיד

אִישׁ מַעֲמִיד אֶת־שִׁמְשׁוֹן

עמד | וַיַּעֲמֵד | הַעֲמֵד | הַעֲמִיד

הֵרִים \ יָרִים

מֹשֶׁה מֵרִים אֶת־יָדוֹ

רום | וַיָּרֶם | הָרֵם | הָרִים

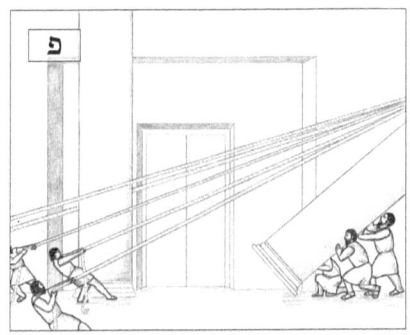

הֵקִים \ יָקִים

אֲנָשִׁים מְקִימִים אֶת־הָעַמּוּדִים

קום | וַיָּקֶם | הָקֵם | הָקִים

---

he'evír / ya'avír
HI: send across
Jacob is sending them across the river. (Gen 32:23)

herím / yarím
HI: lift up; exalt
Moses is lifting up his hand. (Exod 17:11)

he'emíd / ya'amíd
HI: position (cause to stand)
A man is positioning Samson. (Judg 16:25)

heqím / yaqím
HI: raise up; establish
People are raising up the pillars. (2 Chron 3:17)

הֵשִׁיב \ יָשִׁיב

פְּלִשְׁתִּים מְשִׁיבִים אֶת־הָאָרוֹן

שׁוּב | וַיָּשֶׁב | הָשֵׁב | הָשִׁיב

הֵבִיא \ יָבִיא

הָעֹרְבִים מְבִיאִים לֶחֶם לְאֵלִיָּהוּ

בּוֹא | וַיָּבֵא | הָבֵא | הָבִיא

הֵנִיחַ \ יָנִיחַ

מֹשֶׁה מֵנִיחַ אֶת־הַלֻּחוֹת בָּאָרוֹן

נוח | וַיַּנַּח | הַנַּח | הָנִיחַ

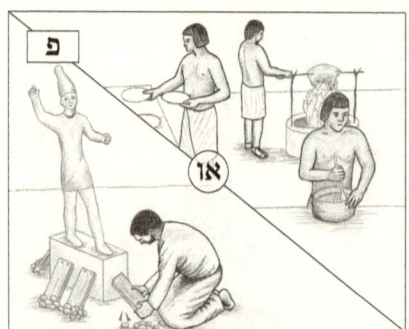

הֵכִין \ יָכִין

מִצְרִים מְכִינִים אֹכֶל לַאֲחֵי־יוֹסֵף

כון | וַיָּכֶן | הָכֵן | הָכִין

heshív / yashív
HI: return (someone/thing)
The Philistines are returning the ark. (1 Sam 6:21)

heví / yaví
HI: bring
The ravens are bringing bread to Elijah. (1 Kgs 17:6)

heníax / yaníax
HI: cause/put to rest
Moses is laying to rest the tablets in the ark. (1 Kgs 8:9)

hexín / yaxín
HI: prepare; make firm
Egyptians are preparing food for Joseph's brothers. (Gen 43:16)

Derived Binyanim

הֶעֱלָה \ יַעֲלֶה

אֲחֵי יוֹסֵף מַעֲלִים אֹתוֹ מִן־הַבּוֹר

עלה | וַיַּעַל | הַעַל | הַעֲלוֹת

הֶרְאָה \ יַרְאֶה

יָעֵל מַרְאָה בָּרָק אֶת־סִיסְרָא

ראה | וַיַּרְא | הַרְאֵה | הַרְאוֹת

הוֹרִיד \ יוֹרִיד

רָחָב מוֹרֶדֶת אֹתָם בְּעַד הַחַלּוֹן

ירד | וַיּוֹרֶד | הוֹרֵד | הוֹרִיד

הוֹצִיא \ יוֹצִיא

יְהוֹשֻׁעַ מוֹצִיא מְלָכִים מֵהַמְּעָרָה

יצא | וַיּוֹצֵא | הוֹצֵא | הוֹצִיא

---

he'elá / ya'alé
HI: bring up; offer up (a sacrifice)
Joseph's brothers are bringing him
up from the cistern. (Gen 37:28)

her'á / yar'é
HI: show
Jael is showing Barak Sisera.
(Judg 4:22)

horíd / yoríd
HI: lower, take down
Rahab is lowering them through the
window. (Josh 2:15)

hotsí / yotsí
HI: bring out
Joshua is bringing out kings from
the cave. (Josh 10:23)

5.4
Pronouns

אֵ֫לֶּה

מָה הָאֲבָנִים הָאֵ֫לֶּה לָכֶם

זֶה \ זֹאת

לָאָ֫רֶץ הַזֹּאת וְלַבַּ֫יִת הַזֶּה

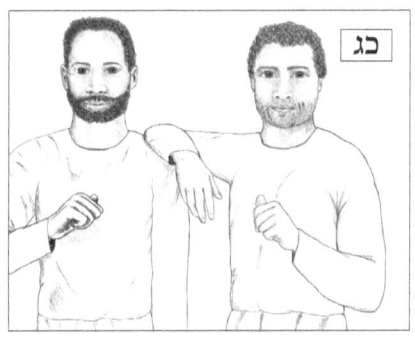

אֲנַ֫חְנוּ

אָ֫נָה אֲנַ֫חְנוּ עֹלִים

אֲנִי · אָנֹכִי

עִבְרִי אָנֹכִי וְאֶת־יְהוָה אֲנִי יָרֵא

---

zé / zót
PRO: this (m/f)
"... to this land and to this house."
(2 Chron 7:21)

éle
PRO: these (c)
"What do these stones mean to you?" (Josh 4:6)

aní / anoxí
PRO: I (c)
"I am a Hebrew, and I fear YHWH."
(Jon 1:9)

anáxnu
PRO: we (c)
"Where are we going up?"
(Deut 1:28)

אַתֶּם

אַתֶּם עֹבְרִים אֶת־הַיַּרְדֵּן

אַתָּה

לֹא־טוֹב הַדָּבָר אֲשֶׁר אַתָּה עֹשֶׂה

אַתֵּן · אַתֵּנָה

וְאַתֵּן צֹאנִי צֹאן מַרְעִיתִי

אַתְּ

וַיֹּאמֶר בַּת־מִי אַתְּ הַגִּידִי נָא לִי

---

atá
PRO: you (ms)
"The thing that you are doing is not good." (Exod 18:17)

át
PRO: you (fs)
And he said, "Whose daughter are you? Please tell me." (Gen 24:23)

atém
PRO: you (mp)
"You are crossing over the Jordan." (Num 33:51)

atén / aténa
PRO: you (fp)
"And you are my flock, the flock of my pasture." (Ezek 34:31)

הוּא

וְהוּא כֹהֵן לְאֵל עֶלְיוֹן

הֵם · הֵׁמָּה

וְהֵם לֹא יָדְעוּ כִּי שֹׁמֵעַ יוֹסֵף

הִיא

כִּי הִיא הָיְתָה אֵם כָּל־חָי

הֵׁנָּה

וַיִּרְאוּ בְנֵי־הָאֱלֹהִים כִּי טֹבֹת הֵׁנָּה

---

hú
PRO: he; that (ms)
And he was priest to God Most High. (Gen 14:18)

hém / héma
PRO: they; those (mp)
And they did not know that Joseph was listening. (Gen 42:23)

hí
PRO: she; that (fs)
... because she was mother of every living person. (Gen 3:20)

héna
PRO: they; those (fp)
And the sons of God saw that they were good. (Gen 6:2)

5.5
Prepositions

Prepositions

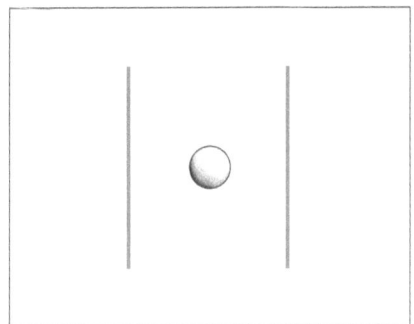

בֵּין

וַיָּשֶׂם לַפִּיד בֵּין־שְׁנֵי הַזְּנָבוֹת

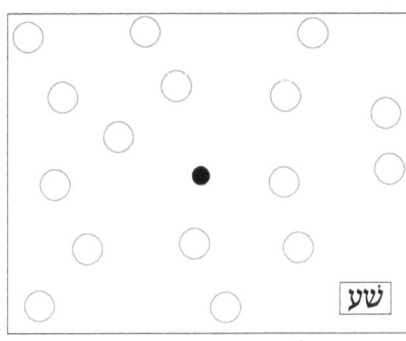

תָּוֶךְ · תּוֹךְ

וּמִפְּרִי הָעֵץ אֲשֶׁר בְּתוֹךְ־הַגָּן

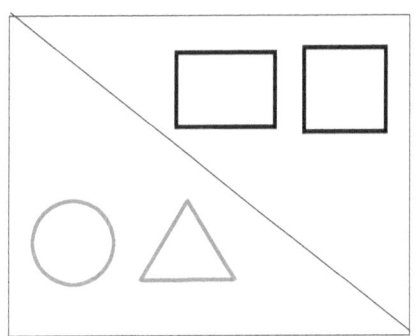

כְּ- · כְּמוֹ

כָּמוֹנִי כָמוֹךָ כְּעַמִּי כְעַמֶּךָ

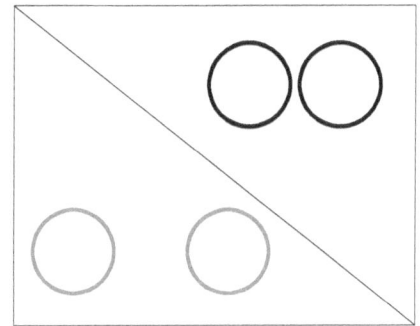

עִם · אֵת

לָמָּה תֵלֵךְ אִתָּנוּ שֵׁב עִם־הַמֶּלֶךְ

---

bén
PREP: between
And he placed a torch between the two tails. (Judg 15:4)

kə / kəmó
PREP: as, like; according to
"I am as you, my people as your people." (1 Kgs 22:4)

távex / tóx
N: middle, midst of
"But from the fruit of the tree in the midst of the garden …" (Gen 3:3)

ím / ét
PREP: with
"Why do you walk with us? Dwell with the king!" (2 Sam 15:19)

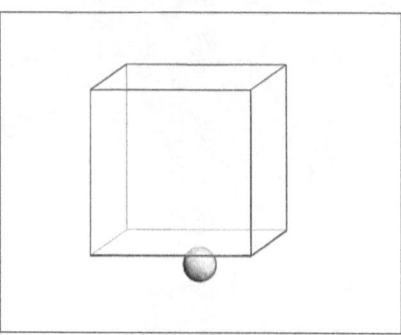

תַּ֫חַת

וְהוּא־עֹמֵד תַּחַת הָעֵץ

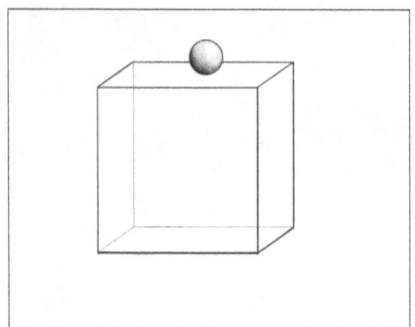

עַל · מֵעַל

וַיָּ֫שֶׂם עַל־הַמִּזְבֵּחַ מִמַּ֫עַל לָעֵצִים

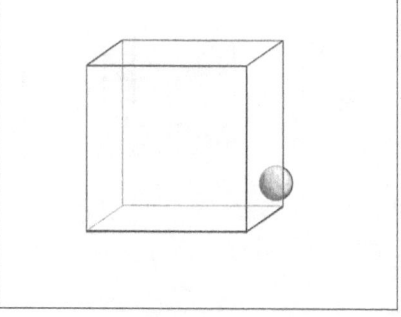

אַחַר · אַחֲרֵי

הִנֵּה עַבְדְּךָ יַעֲקֹב אַחֲרֵינוּ

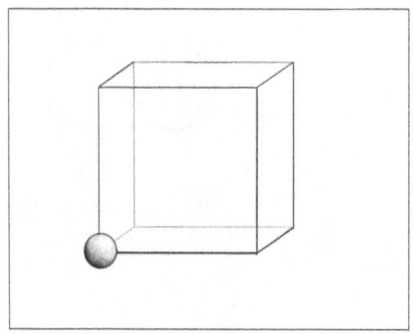

לִפְנֵי

וַאֲבָרֶכְךָ לִפְנֵי יְהוָה לִפְנֵי מוֹתִי

ál / má'al
PREP: on, above; against; about
And he placed (him) on the altar on top of the wood. (Gen 22:9)

táxat
PREP: under; instead of
And he was standing under the tree. (Gen 18:8)

lifné
PREP: in front of, before
"And I shall bless you in front of YHWH before I die." (Gen 27:7)

axár / axaré
PREP: behind, after
"Behold, your servant Jacob is behind us." (Gen 32:21*)

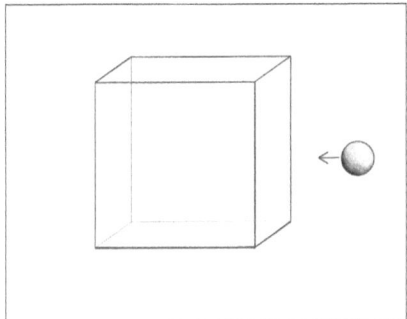

אֶל · -לְ

וַיֹּאמֶר לָהּ שׁוּבִי אֶל־גְּבִרְתֵּךְ

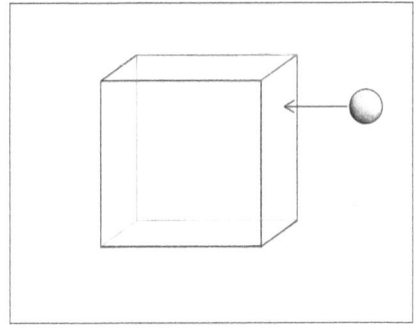

עַד

עַד־בֹּאֲכֶם עַד־הַמָּקוֹם הַזֶּה

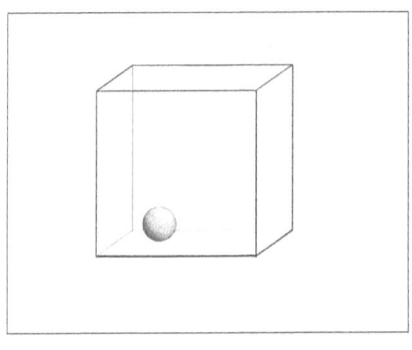

-בְּ

אָכֵן יֵשׁ יְהוָה בַּמָּקוֹם הַזֶּה

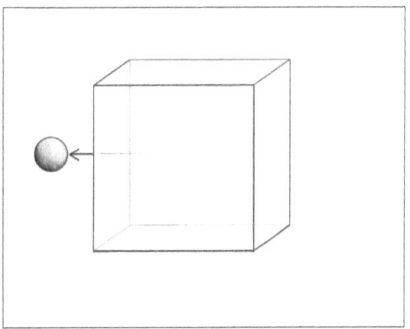

מִן

וַיִּקְרָא מַלְאַךְ יְהוָה מִן־הַשָּׁמַיִם

---

lə / él
PREP: to, toward, for
And he said to her, "Return to your mistress!" (Gen 16:9)

bə
PREP: in, by; with; against
"Surely YHWH is in this place." (Gen 28:16)

ád
PREP: until; while, during
"... until you came up to this place." (Deut 1:31)

mín
PREP: from, out; than; because
And the angel of YHWH cried out from heaven. (Gen 22:11)

5.6
Question Words

Question Words 153

מִי

וַיֹּאמֶר לוֹ יִצְחָק אָבִיו מִי־אַתָּה

מָה

וַיִּקְרָא פַרְעֹה מַה־זֹּאת עָשִׂיתָ לִּי

הֲ־

הֲשֹׁמֵר אָחִי אָנֹכִי

Why?

לָמָה

לָמָה לֹא־הִגַּדְתָּ לִּי כִּי אִשְׁתְּךָ הִיא

---

mí
PRO: Who?
And Isaac his father said to him,
"Who are you?" (Gen 27:32)

má
PRO: What?
Pharaoh called out, "What is this
you have done to me?" (Gen 12:18)

ha
(indicator of yes/no question)
"Am I the keeper of my brother?"
(Gen 4:9)

láma
Why?
"Why did you not tell me that she is
your wife?" (Gen 12:18)

5.7
English Translations

English Translations

אוֹ	or	כִּי	because, that; but
אָז	ADV: then, at that time	כִּי אִם	except, but rather
אֵין	there is not	כֵּן	ADV: thus, so
אַךְ	but, only	לֹא	no, not
אַל	no, not	לְבַד	ADV: alone, besides
אִם	if	לָכֵן	therefore
אָמַר	Q: say	לְמַעַן	PREP: on account of; in order that (with inf.)
אַף	even, indeed		
אֲשֶׁר	who, that, which	מְאֹד	ADV: very
אֵת	object marker	מָלַךְ	Q: reign
בִּלְתִּי	no, not	מְעַט	ADV: little, few
בְּעַד	PREP: behind; for	מַעֲשֶׂה	N: deed, action
גָּדַל	Q: grow up, be great	מַרְאֶה	N: appearance
גַּם	ADV: also, even	נָא	please
הַ	the	נָבִיא	N: prophet
הָיָה	Q: be, become; happen	נֶגֶד	PREP: opposite, in front
הֵן	behold, look	עוֹד	ADV: again, still, yet
הִנֵּה	behold, look	עָשָׂה	Q: do, make
וְ	and; but, then	פֹּה	ADV: here
חָזַק	Q: be strong	פֶּן	lest, or else
חָיָה	Q: live, be alive	פַּעַם	N: time (occurrence)
יַחַד	ADV: together	קָדַשׁ	Q: be holy
יַחְדָּו	ADV: together	רָבָה	Q: be(come) many
יַעַן	PREP: on account of	רַע	Q: be bad, be evil
יֵשׁ	there is	רַק	ADV: only
כַּאֲשֶׁר	just as	שֶׁ	who, that, which
כֹּה	ADV: thus, here	שָׁם	ADV: there

GLOSSARY

א

אָב	father 60	אַךְ	but 155
אָבַד	perish 97	אָכַל	eat 49
אֶבֶן	stone 27	אַל	not 155
אֱדוֹם	Edom 92	אֵל	God 80
אָדוֹן	master 63	אֶל	toward 151
אָדָם	humankind 42	אֵלֶּה	these 145
אֲדָמָה	ground 24	אֶלֶף	thousand 119
אָהַב	love 134	אֵם	mother 60
אֹהֶל	tent 108	אִם	if 155
אוֹ	or 155	אַמָּה	cubit 111
אוֹר	light 21	אָמַר	say 155
אָז	then 155	אֱמֶת	truth 66
אֹזֶן	ear 45	אֲנִי	I 145
אָח	brother 61	אֲנַחְנוּ	we 145
אֶחָד	one 116	אָסַף	gather 131
אָחוֹת	sister 61	אַף	nose 45
אַחַר	after 150	אַף	indeed 155
אַחֵר	another 114	אֵפוֹד	ephod 54
אֹיֵב	enemy 96	אֶצְבַּע	finger 44
אַיִל	ram 31	אַרְבַּע	four 117
אֵין	there is not 155	אָרוֹן	chest 77
אֵיפָה	ephah 111	אַרְיֵה	lion 33
אִישׁ	man 41	אֹרֶךְ	length 112
		אֲרָם	Aram 93

אֶרֶץ	land 22	בֵּן	understand 99
אֵשׁ	fire 25	בֵּן	son 61
אִשָּׁה	woman 41	בָּנָה	build 107
אַשּׁוּר	Assyria 93	בְּעַד	through 155
אֲשֶׁר	which 155	בַּעַל	owner 72
אַתְּ	you (fs) 146	בָּקָר	cattle 30
אֵת	with 149	בֹּקֶר	morning 37
אֵת	object marker 155	בִּקֵּשׁ	seek 65
אַתָּה	you (ms) 146	בְּרִית	covenant 86
אַתֶּם	you (mp) 146	בֵּרַךְ	bless 88
אַתֵּן	you (fp) 146	בֶּרֶךְ	knee 44
		בָּשָׂר	meat 50
	ב	בַּת	daughter 61
בְּ	in 151		
בָּא	come 123		ג
בָּבֶל	Babylon 93	גָּאַל	redeem 59
בֶּגֶד	clothing 54	גְּבוּל	border 91
בְּהֵמָה	livestock 30	גִּבּוֹר	warrior 96
בּוֹא	(root of בָּא)	גָּדוֹל	big 113
בּוֹשׁ	be embarrassed 135	גָּדַל	be great 155
בָּחַר	choose 130	גּוֹי	nation 83
בָּטַח	trust 135	גָּלָה	depart 127
בִּין	(root of בֵּן)	גָּלָה	uncover 53
בֵּין	between 149	גִּלְעָד	Gilead 92
בַּיִת	house 105	גַּם	also 155
בָּכָה	cry 134	גָּמָל	camel 32
בְּכוֹר	firstborn 62		
בָּלַע	swallow 49		ד
בִּלְתִּי	not 155	דִּבֶּר	speak 101
בָּמָה	high place 77	דּוֹר	generation 60

Hebrew	English	Page
דֶּלֶת	door	106
דָּם	blood	78
דֶּרֶךְ	path	108
דָּרַשׁ	inquire	85
דֶּשֶׁא	grass	29

ה

Hebrew	English	Page
הַ	the	155
הֲ	question mark	155
הֵבִיא	bring	142
הֵבִין	explain	99
הִגִּיד	tell	67
הוּא	he	147
הוֹדָה	thank	81
הוֹלִיד	beget	59
הוֹלִיךְ	lead	89
הוֹצִיא	bring out	143
הוֹרִיד	lower	143
הוֹשִׁיעַ	save	89
הֶחֱזִיק	hold tightly	140
הֵחֵל	begin	132
הִיא	she	147
הָיָה	be	155
הֵיכָל	temple	76
הִין	hin	111
הִכָּה	strike	95
הֵכִין	prepare	142
הִכְרִית	cut off	140
הָלַךְ	walk	125
הִלֵּל	praise	81
הֵם	they (m)	147
הֵמִית	kill	97
הֵן	behold	155
הֵנָּה	they (f)	147
הִנֵּה	behold	155
הֵנִיחַ	give rest	142
הֵסִיר	remove	53
הֶעֱבִיר	send across	141
הֶעֱלָה	bring up	143
הֶעֱמִיד	position	141
הִצִּיל	rescue	89
הִקְטִיר	make smoke	75
הֵקִים	raise up	141
הִקְרִיב	bring near	140
הַר	mountain	25
הֶרְאָה	show	143
הִרְבָּה	multiply	59
הָרַג	slay	95
הֵרִים	lift up	141
הֵרַע	do evil	73
הֵשִׁיב	return	142
הִשְׁלִיךְ	throw	130
הִשְׁמִיעַ	proclaim	140
הִשְׁתַּחֲוָה	bow down	81
הִתְהַלֵּךְ	walk about	109
הִתְהַלֵּל	boast	137
הִתְחַזֵּק	strengthen self	137

ו

Hebrew	English	Page
וְ	and	155

ז

זֹאת	this (fs)	145
זֶבַח	sacrifice	75
זֶבַח	sacrifice	74
זֶה	this (ms)	145
זָהָב	gold	27
זָכַר	remember	87
זָקֵן	elder	42
זֶרַע	seed	51

ח

חֶדֶר	room	106
חֹדֶשׁ	month	36
חוה	(root of הִשְׁתַּחֲוָה)	
חוֹמָה	wall (city)	105
חוּץ	outside	77
חָזַק	be strong	155
חִזֵּק	strengthen	138
חָטָא	sin	73
חַטָּאת	sin	72
חַי	living	79
חָיָה	live	155
חַיָּה	animal	30
חִיָּה	let live	139
חַיִל	wealth	80
חָכָם	wise	79
חַלּוֹן	window	106
חִלֵּל	profane	73
חֵמָה	wrath	66
חֲמוֹר	donkey	32
חָמֵשׁ	five	117
חֲמִשָּׁה	fifty	119
חָנָה	encamp	109
חֶסֶד	steadfast love	86
חָסֵר	be lacking	133
חֲצִי	half	112
חָצֵר	courtyard	76
חֹק	statute	84
חֻקָּה	statute	84
חֶרֶב	sword	94
חָשַׁב	think	99

ט

טַבַּעַת	ring	55
טוֹב	good	71
טָמֵא	be unclean	73
טַעַם	taste	49

י

יָד	hand	43
ידה	(root of הוֹדָה)	
יָדַע	know	99
יְהוָה	YHWH	80
יוֹם	day	37
יַחַד	together	155
יַיִן	wine	51
יָכֹל	be able	135
יָלַד	give birth	59
יֶלֶד	boy	41
יַלְדָּה	girl	41

יָם	sea	23	כָּלָה	be finished	107
יָמִין	right hand	43	כִּלָּה	finish	132
יָסַף	add	115	כְּלִי	vessel	55
יַעַן	on account of	155	כְּמוֹ	like	149
יָצָא	go out	123	כֵּן	thus	155
יָרֵא	fear	135	כָּנָף	wing	33
יָרַד	go down	125	כִּסֵּא	chair	100
יַרְדֵּן	Jordan	22	כִּסָּה	cover	53
יְרוּשָׁלַם	Jerusalem	91	כֶּסֶף	silver	27
יָרַשׁ	take possession	95	כַּף	palm	43
יִשְׂרָאֵל	Israel	91	כִּפֶּר	atone	75
יֵשׁ	there is	155	כָּרַת	cut	87
יָשַׁב	sit	124	כָּתַב	write	101
ישׁע	(root of הוֹשִׁיעַ)		כָּתֵף	shoulder	44
יָשָׁר	straight	79			

כ

כְּ	as	149
כַּאֲשֶׁר	just as	155
כָּבֵד	heavy	113
כִּבֵּד	honor	139
כָּבוֹד	glory	80
כֶּבֶשׂ	sheep	31
כֹּה	thus	155
כֹּהֵן	priest	78
כון	(root of נָכוֹן)	
כֹּחַ	strength	47
כִּי	because	155
כִּי אִם	except	155
כֹּל	all	112

ל

לְ	to	151
לֹא	not	155
לֵב	heart	47
לְבַד	alone	155
לָבַשׁ	wear	53
לחם	(root of נִלְחַם)	
לֶחֶם	bread	50
לַיְלָה	night	37
לָכַד	seize	130
לָכֵן	therefore	155
לָמָּה	why?	153
לְמַעַן	in order that	155
לִפְנֵי	in front of	150
לָקַח	take	129

Glossary

לִקְרַאת	meet	69
לָשׁוֹן	tongue	46

מ

מְאֹד	very	155
מֵאָה	hundred	119
מְגִלָּה	scroll	100
מִגְרָשׁ	pastureland	24
מִדְבָּר	desert	25
מָה	what?	153
מוֹאָב	Moab	92
מוֹעֵד	appointed place	77
מוּת	(root of מֵת)	
מִזְבֵּחַ	altar	74
מַחֲנֶה	camp	94
מַטֶּה	staff	62
מִי	who?	153
מַיִם	water	23
מָכַר	sell	115
מָלֵא	be full	133
מִלֵּא	fill	138
מַלְאָךְ	messenger	68
מְלָאכָה	occupation	86
מִלְחָמָה	battle	94
מָלַךְ	reign	155
מֶלֶךְ	king	83
מַמְלָכָה	kingdom	83
מִן	from	151
מִנְחָה	gift	74
מִסְפָּר	number	116
מְעַט	few	155
מְעִיל	coat	54
מַעַל	above	150
מַעֲשֶׂה	action	155
מָצָא	find	65
מִצְוָה	commandment	84
מִצְרַיִם	Egypt	93
מָקוֹם	location	24
מַקֵּל	stick	29
מַרְאֶה	appearance	155
מִשְׁכָּן	tabernacle	76
מִשְׁפָּחָה	family	60
מִשְׁפָּט	judgment	84
מִשְׁתֶּה	feast	50
מֵת	die	97

נ

נָא	please	155
נְאֻם	declaration	68
נִבָּא	prophesy	67
נָבִיא	prophet	155
נֶגֶב	Negev	22
נגד	(root of הִגִּיד)	
נֶגֶד	opposite	155
נָגַע	touch	132
נָהָר	river	23
נוח	(root of נָח)	
נוס	(root of נָס)	
נָח	rest	107
נַחַל	stream	23

נַחֲלָה	inheritance............62	סֵפֶר	document............100
נִחַם	relent 88	סִפֵּר	recount................67
נִחַם	comfort...............139	סָר	turn aside............123
נָחָשׁ	snake 33		
נְחֹשֶׁת	bronze.................27		**ע**
נָטָה	stretch out............69	עָבַד	work 107
נכה	(root of הִכָּה)	עֶבֶד	slave 63
נָכוֹן	be ready.............133	עֲבֹדָה	service 78
נִלְחַם	fight 95	עָבַר	pass over............126
נִמְצָא	be found 137	עֵגֶל	calf.....................31
נָס	flee....................127	עֲגָלָה	wagon...............108
נָסַע	journey 109	עַד	until 151
נַעַל	sandal 55	עֵדָה	congregation........68
נַעַר	young man..........42	עוֹד	again..................155
נָפַל	fall 133	עוֹלָם	forever 35
נֶפֶשׁ	soul 86	עָוֹן	transgression 72
נצל	(root of הִצִּיל)	עוֹף	bird(s).................33
נִרְאָה	appear................137	עֵז	goat....................32
נָשָׂא	pick up...............129	עָזַב	leave 130
נָשִׂיא	leader..................63	עֲטָרָה	crown..................55
נִשְׁאַר	remain 127	עַיִן	eye......................45
נִשְׁבַּע	swear 67	עִיר	city....................105
נָתַן	give...................129	עַל	on......................150
		עָלָה	go up.................125
	ס	עֹלָה	burnt offering 74
סָבַב	go around 126	עַם	people.................83
סָגַר	shut...................131	עִם	with 149
סוּס	horse...................32	עָמַד	stand 124
סוּר	(root of סָר)	עַמּוּד	pillar...................76
סָפַר	count.................115	עַמּוֹן	Ammon 92

עָנָב	grape 51		צַדִּיק	righteous 71
עָנָה	answer 65		צִוָּה	command 85
עָפָר	dust 25		צָפוֹן	north 22
עֵץ	tree 29			
עֶצֶם	bone 47		**ק**	
עֶרֶב	evening 37		קָבַר	bury 97
עָשָׂה	do 155		קָדוֹשׁ	holy 79
עֶשְׂרֵה	teen 118		קָדַשׁ	be holy 155
עֶשֶׂר	ten 118		קִדֵּשׁ	consecrate 138
עֶשְׂרִים	twenty 119		קָהָל	assembly 68
עֵת	time 35		קוֹל	voice 66
עַתָּה	now 35		קוּם	(root of קָם)
			קוֹמָה	height 112
	פ		קִיר	wall (house) 106
פֶּה	mouth 45		קִלֵּל	curse 88
פֹּה	here 155		קָם	get up 124
פֶּן	lest 155		קָנָה	buy 115
פָּנָה	turn 126		קָרָא	call out 101
פָּנִים	face 46		קָרַב	come near 126
פַּעַם	occurrence 155		קֶרֶב	entrails 47
פָּקַד	visit 69			
פַּר	bull 31		**ר**	
פֶּרַח	flower 29		רָאָה	see 132
פְּרִי	fruit 51		רֹאשׁ	head 44
פָּתַח	open 131		רִאשׁוֹן	first 114
פֶּתַח	opening 108		רַב	many 113
			רָבָה	become many 155
	צ		רֶגֶל	foot 43
צֹאן	flock 30		רָדַף	chase 127
צָבָא	army 96		רוּחַ	spirit 21

Glossary 163

Glossary

רוֹם	(root of רָם)		שָׁב	return 123
רוּץ	(root of רָץ)		שָׁבוּעַ	week 36
רֹחַב	width 112		שֵׁבֶט	rod 62
רֶכֶב	chariot(s) 94		שבע	(root of נִשְׁבַּע)
רָם	be high 81		שֶׁבַע	seven 117
רָעַ	be evil 155		שָׁבַר	break 87
רַע	evil 71		שַׁבָּת	Sabbath 36
רֵעַ	neighbor 63		שׁוּב	(root of שָׁב)
רָעָב	famine 50		שָׁחַת	destroy 88
רֹעֶה	shepherd 89		שָׁכַב	lie down 124
רעע	(root of רַע)		שָׁכַח	forget 87
רָץ	run 125		שָׁכַן	dwell 109
רַק	only 155		שָׁלוֹם	peace 66
רָשָׁע	wicked 71		שָׁלוֹשׁ	three 116
			שָׁלַח	send 69
	שׂ		שִׁלַּח	send away 139
שָׂדֶה	field 24		שֻׁלְחָן	table 100
שִׂים	(root of שָׂם)		שְׁלִישִׁי	third 114
שָׂם	set down 129		שלך	(root of הִשְׁלִיךְ)
שָׂמַח	be happy 134		שָׁלֵם	whole 113
שִׂמְלָה	garment 54		שִׁלֵּם	(re)pay 138
שָׂנֵא	hate 134		שָׁם	there 155
שָׂפָה	lip 46		שֵׁם	name 42
שַׂר	commander 96		שָׁמַיִם	heaven 21
שָׂרַף	burn 75		שֶׁמֶן	oil 78
			שְׁמֹנֶה	eight 118
	שׁ		שָׁמַע	hear 101
שֶׁ	which 155		שָׁמַר	keep 85
שָׁאַל	ask 65		שֹׁמְרוֹן	Samaria 91
שאר	(root of נִשְׁאַר)		שֶׁמֶשׁ	sun 21

שֵׁן	tooth	46	שָׁתָה	drink	49
שָׁנָה	year	36			

ת

שֵׁנִי	second	114
שְׁנַיִם	two	116
שַׁעַר	gate	105
שָׁפַט	judge	85
שָׁפַךְ	pour out	131
שֶׁקֶל	shekel	111
שֶׁקֶר	lie	66
שֵׁשׁ	six	117

תָּוֶךְ	midst	149
תּוֹעֵבָה	abomination	72
תּוֹרָה	law	84
תַּחַת	under	150
תָּמִיד	continually	35
תֵּשַׁע	nine	118

ENGLISH INDEX

abomination 72
above 150
action 155
add 115
again 155
all 112
alone 155
also 155
altar 74
Ammon 92
and 155
animal 30
another 114
answer 65
appear 137
appearance 155
appointed place 77
Aram 93
army 96
as 149
ask 65
assembly 68
Assyria 93
atone 75

Babylon 93
battle 94
be 155
be able 135
be embarrassed 135
be evil 155
be finished 107
be found 137
be full 133
be great 155
be happy 134
be high 81
be holy 155
be lacking 133
be ready 133
be strong 155
be unclean 73
be(come) many 155
because 155
beget 59
begin 132
behind 150
behold 155
between 149

big	113
bird(s)	33
bless	88
blood	78
boast	137
bone	47
border	91
bow down	81
boy	41
bread	50
break	87
bring	142
bring near	140
bring out	143
bring up	143
bronze	27
brother	61
build	107
bull	31
burn	75
bury	97
but	155
buy	115
calf	31
call out	101
camel	32
camp	94
cattle	30
chair	100
chariot(s)	94
chase	127
chest	77
choose	130
city	105
clothing	54
coat	54
come	123
come near	126
comfort	139
command	85
commander	96
commandment	84
congregation	68
consecrate	138
continually	35
count	115
courtyard	76
covenant	86
cover	53
crown	55
cry	134
cubit	111
curse	88
cut	87
cut off	140
daughter	61
day	37
declaration	68
depart	127
desert	25
destroy	88
die	97

do	155	field	24
do evil	73	fifty	119
document	100	fight	95
donkey	32	fill	138
door	106	find	65
drink	49	finger	44
dust	25	finish	132
dwell	109	fire	25
ear	45	first	114
eat	49	firstborn	62
Edom	92	five	117
Egypt	93	flee	127
eight	118	flock	30
encamp	109	flower	29
enemy	96	foot	43
entrails	47	forever	35
ephah	111	forget	87
ephod	54	four	117
evening	37	from	151
evil	155	fruit	51
except	155	garment	54
explain	99	gate	105
eye	45	gather	131
face	46	generation	60
fall	133	get up	124
family	60	gift	74
famine	50	Gilead	92
father	60	girl	41
fear	135	give	129
feast	50	give birth	59
few	155	glory	80

English Index 169

go around	126
go down	125
go out	123
go up	125
goat	32
God	80
gold	27
good	71
grape	51
grass	29
ground	24
guard	85
half	112
hand	43
hate	134
he	147
head	44
hear	101
heart	47
heaven	21
heavy	113
height	112
here	155
high place	77
hin	111
hold tightly	140
holy	79
honor	139
horse	32
house	105
humankind	42
hundred	119
I	145
if	155
in	151
in front of	150
in order that	155
indeed	155
inheritance	62
inquire	85
Israel	91
Jerusalem	91
Jordan	22
journey	109
judge	85
judgment	84
just as	155
kill	97
king	83
kingdom	83
knee	44
know	99
land	22
law	84
lead	89
leader	63
leave	130
length	112
lest	155
let live	139
lie	66
lie down	124

light	21
like	149
lion	33
lip	46
live	155
livestock	30
living	79
location	24
love	134
lower	143
make smoke	75
man	41
many	113
master	63
meat	50
meet	69
messenger	68
midst	149
Moab	92
month	36
morning	37
mother	60
mountain	25
mouth	45
multiply	59
name	42
nation	83
Negev	22
neighbor	63
night	37
nine	118

north	22
nose	45
not	155
now	35
number	116
(object marker)	155
occupation	86
occurrence	155
oil	78
old	42
on	150
on account of	155
one	116
only	155
open	131
opening	108
opposite	155
or	155
outside	77
owner	72
palm	43
pass over	126
pastureland	24
peace	66
people	83
perish	97
pick up	129
pillar	76
please	155
position	141
pour out	131

praise	81
prepare	142
priest	78
proclaim	140
profane	73
prophesy	67
prophet	155
put on	53
(question mark)	143
raise up	141
ram	31
recount	67
redeem	59
reign	155
relent	88
remain	127
remember	87
remove	53
repay	138
rescue	89
rest	107
rest (causative)	142
return	123
return (causative)	142
right hand	43
righteous	71
ring	55
river	23
road	108
rod	117
room	106
run	125
Sabbath	36
sacrifice (noun)	74
sacrifice (verb)	75
Samaria	91
sandal	55
save	89
say	155
scroll	100
sea	23
second	114
see	132
seed	51
seek	65
seize	130
sell	115
send	69
send across	141
send away	139
service	78
set down	129
seven	117
she	147
sheep	31
shekel	111
shepherd	89
shoulder	44
show	143
shut	131
silver	27
sin (noun)	72

sin (verb)	73
sister	61
sit	124
six	117
slave	63
slay	95
snake	33
son	61
soul	86
speak	101
staff	62
stand	124
statute	84
steadfast love	86
stick	29
stone	27
straight	79
stream	23
strength	47
strengthen	138
strengthen self	137
stretch out	69
strike	95
sun	21
swallow	49
swear	67
sword	94
tabernacle	76
table	100
take	129
take possession of	95
taste	49
teen	118
tell	67
temple	76
ten	118
tent	108
thank	81
the	155
then	155
there	155
there is	155
there is not	155
therefore	155
these	145
they (f)	147
they (m)	147
think	99
third	114
this (fs)	145
this (ms)	145
thousand	119
three	116
through	155
throw	130
thus, here	155
thus, in this way	155
time	35
to	151
together	155
tongue	46
tooth	46

English Index

touch 132
toward 151
transgression 72
tree 29
trust 135
truth 66
turn 126
turn aside 123
twenty 119
two 116
uncover 53
under 150
understand 99
until 151
very 155
vessel 55
visit 69
voice 66
wagon 108
walk 125
walk about 109
wall (city) 105
wall (house) 106
warrior 96
water 23
we 145
wealth 80

week 36
what? 153
which 155
who? 153
whole 113
whole burnt offering 74
why? 153
wicked 71
width 112
wind 21
window 106
wine 51
wing 33
wise 79
with 149
woman 41
work 78
wrath 66
write 101
year 36
YHWH 80
you (fs) 146
you (fp) 146
you (ms) 146
you (mp) 146
young man 42

www.ingramcontent.com/pod-product-compliance
Lightning Source LLC
Chambersburg PA
CBHW030328100526
44592CB00010B/618